MONROE COLLEGE LIBRARY

3 7340 01073398 5

Presentation Skills for Managers

WITHDRAWN from
Monroe College Library

Other titles in the Briefcase Books series include:

To learn more about titles in the Briefcase Books series go to
www.briefcasebooks.com
You'll find the tables of contents, downloadable sample chapters, information about the authors, discussion guides for using these books in training programs, and more.

Presentation Skills for Managers

Jennifer Rotondo
Mike Rotondo

McGraw-Hill

New York Chicago San Francisco Lisbon Madrid
Mexico City Milan New Delhi San Juan
Seoul Singapore Sydney Toronto

57/8.22
·R68
2002

McGraw-Hill

A Division of The **McGraw·Hill** *Companies*

Copyright © 2002 by The McGraw-Hill Companies, Inc. All rights reserved.
Printed in the United States of America. Except as permitted under the
United States Copyright Act of 1976, no part of this publication may be
reproduced or distributed in any form or by any means, or stored in a data-
base or retrieval system, without the prior written permission of the publisher.

1 2 3 4 5 6 7 8 9 0 AGM/AGM 0 9 8 7 6 5 4 3 2 1

ISBN 0-07-137930-4

This is a CWL Publishing Enterprises Book, *developed and produced for*
McGraw-Hill by CWL Publishing Enterprises, *John A. Woods, President. For*
more information, contact CWL Publishing Enterprises, 3010 Irvington Way,
Madison, WI 53713-3414, www.cwlpub.com. Robert Magnan served as editor.
For McGraw-Hill, the sponsoring editor is Catherine Dassopoulos, and the
publisher is Jeffrey Krames.

Printed and bound by Quebecor World.

This publication is designed to provide accurate and authoritative information in regard to the subject matter covered. It is sold with the understanding
that neither the author nor the publisher is engaged in rendering legal,
accounting, or other professional service. If legal advice or other expert
assistance is required, the services of a competent professional person
should be sought.
> —*From a Declaration of Principles jointly adopted by a Committee*
> *of the American Bar Association and a Committee of Publishers*

McGraw-Hill books are available at special quantity discounts to use as pre-
miums and sale promotions, or for use in corporate training programs. For
more information, please write to the Director of Special Sales, McGraw-Hill,
2 Penn Plaza, New York, NY 10121. Or contact your local bookstore.

This book is printed on recycled, acid-free paper containing a mini-
mum of 50% recycled de-inked fiber.

Contents

Preface

"How do I create and deliver an effective presentation?" Perhaps you've asked yourself this question at least a few times and that's what draws you to this book. You strive to create a memorable, maybe even great, presentation, but somehow it doesn't turn out that way. You may have some ideas about how to create this caliber of presentation, but there's no "official" training available for individuals like you to learn the guidelines for creating an effective presentation.

That's where we fit in. For many years, we've been teaching people in every type of organiation how to plan create, and deliver speeches, talks, and presentations that move and help people. What we teach is what you'll find in this book—a series of simple, easy-to-follow techniques that work.

This book is designed to walk you through a step-by-step process that will help you make your next presentation the best you've ever done. We discuss presentation guidelines and give you our tips and techniques to make you more efficient. Plus, we discuss in depth how to use the most popular presentation software package out there, Microsoft PowerPoint. In fact, this is one of the only books available that combines presentation how-to with the secrets of creating great PowerPoint slides to go with your talk.

Overview

This process is broken down into three phases—content, design, and delivery—in Chapter 1. In Chapter 2, we first discuss how to do research. Then, we outline ways to organize and arrange your material. Finally, we pull all of this information together into our presentation outline.

After we have our outline, we convert it into a slide presentation in Chapter 3. We discuss guidelines for creating effective bullets, designing appropriate text layout, preparing the proper number of slides, and using graphics to further enhance the impact of your presentation. We take all of these steps before we even open PowerPoint.

Then, we get into the nitty-gritty of efficiently using the application to implement our design plans. Chapter 4 goes into great detail about PowerPoint and how to use it effectively, emphasizing the three keys to a professional presentation—layout, consistency, and color. You'll learn about how to lay out your slides properly, what type of fonts to use, how to select appropriate images and charts, and how to determine the right colors for your presentation. Chapter 5 is all about creating high-impact design. We cover the three focal points for a presentation—audience, image, and objective.

Chapter 6 will help you take your simple point presentation and add pizzazz. We discuss the six ways to add flavor and excitement in PowerPoint: symbols, clip art, photos, charts, sound, and videos. We go into great detail on how to insert and manipulate each one of these elements.

Finally, we reach the delivery phase. This starts with Chapter 7—The Presentation Environment and Logistics. This chapter discusses the setting, lighting, room equipment, and acoustics. Chapter 8 is all about facilitation skills. This chapter is filled with tips and techniques for getting and keeping your audience's attention. Chapters 9 and 10 cover such aspects of delivery as managing nervousness, setting up for your presentation, making a great first impression, using body language, working with your slides, handling questions, and dealing with disasters.

In Chapter 11, we discuss how to determine the success of your presentation. You'll ask yourself questions like "Did I meet the objective of my presentation?" and "How well did I handle audience feedback?" This is the chapter that helps you learn from your presentation so the next one will be even better.

Finally, there's a bonus: an appendix that lists tips for using PowerPoint. This is the practical section for those in a hurry to put PowerPoint to work.

Special Features

The idea behind the books in the Briefcase Series is to give you practical information written in a friendly person-to-person style. The chapters are short, deal with tactical issues, and include lots of examples. They also feature numerous boxes designed to give you different types of specific information. Here's a description of the boxes you'll find in this book.

 These boxes do just what they say: give you tips and tactics for being smart in the way in which you plan and deliver and your presentation.

 These boxes provide warnings for where things could go wrong during every phase of the presentation process.

 Here you'll find the kind of how-to hints the pros use to make your presentation go as smoothly as possible.

 Every activity has its special jargon and terms. These boxes provide definitions of these concepts.

 Look for these boxes for examples of principles and practices described in the text.

 Here you'll find specific procedures and techniques you can use to create a great presentation.

How can you make sure you won't make a mistake sometime during the presentation process? You can't. But if you see a box like this, it will give you practical advice on how to minimize the possibility.

Acknowledgments

Writing a book is always a collaborative process. We have many people to thank for their generous support. First and foremost, we extend warm appreciation to John Woods of CWL Publishing Enterprises, for his invaluable guidance, patience, and belief in this project and in us. And thanks to Bob Magnan, also with CWL, whose editing skills and encouraging words were both greatly valued. Susan Dees was a terrific source of creative inspiration, always willing to talk through a new idea or concept. Maggie Kaeter was there with priceless support as our deadline approached. Carol's husband, Steven, deserves special credit for his unfaltering support demonstrated in ways too numerous to mention. We offer a special thank you to our friends at Canyon of the Eagles Nature Park and Lodge—especially Michael J. Scott, who helped us stay true to our target read-ers—and to the numerous other friends and family members who told us "we know you can do it."

About the Authors

Jennifer Rotondo is a Microsoft certified "PowerPoint Expert." She utilizes her abundance of knowledge in her Advanced PowerPoint Seminar and in several publications including:

- *PowerPoint 2000: Getting Professional Results*, a Microsoft publication detailing its new features
- *Point, Click and Wow!*, A Guide to Brilliant Laptop Presentations
- *Understanding Computers*, a textbook for lower-division college students

She contributes a monthly column to Presentations magazine in which she critiques subscribers' presentations.

She also designs high-tech presentation tools for businesses. She takes projects from start to finish, providing smart design and logical layout, helping businesses inform, persuade and educate their audiences through presentation design. Visit her Web site at www.creativemindsinc.com.

Mike Rotondo has over 23 years of management experience in the restaurant and retail environment. He has 13+ years in multi-unit management. He is currently a regional manager with the HoneyBaked Ham Company of Georgia. Before HoneyBaked, Mike worked with Wendy's International for 8 years, where he received his certification as a trainer and meeting facilitator. Mike's specialty is in creating sales initiatives and motivation speeches.

What Makes a Great Presentation?

M any people ask themselves the question in this chapter's title. Is it in the way you create the content? Is it in the way you put the pieces together? Is it in the way you deliver the presentation?

I know that you'd agree that there have been times when you went to a presentation or a company meeting, only to walk away feeling that it was a total waste of time. It was not a great presentation. But why?

Actually, a great presentation is a combination of the three elements: content, design, and delivery. Stay focused and use what's presented in this book and you will severely lessen the chance that your participants will walk away after one of your presentations with the feeling that it was a total waste of time. This book was specifically written to help you create a great presentation.

Content, Design, and Delivery

There are three elements to a great presentation: content, design, and delivery. *Content* includes the research and organization of

> **Key Term**
>
> **Presentation** A visual and aural event intended to communicate, for the purposes of providing information, helping to understand, gaining agreement, and/or motivating to act. That's a rough, general definition. Some guides will divide presentations according to the purpose—motivational, informational, persuasive, and so forth. Although your purposes should determine many choices that you'll make, any presentation requires proper attention to the three basics: content, design, and delivery.

materials. *Design* is the architecture of the slides and the graphical enhancements. *Delivery* is how you voice your message. To make the presentation great, there must be synergy of these three elements. Each of these elements carries equal weight and importance. Your presentation will not be great unless you have all three of these elements.

For example, let's say you don't do a good job researching and organizing your content, but you spend hours designing the presentation with all the bells and whistles and hours practicing your delivery. What's going to happen when you get in front of your audience? You're going to run through your presentation and it won't be interactive because you don't know more than what's on your slides. Your audience is going to pay attention to the next sound or wild animation. When someone asks you questions, you're not going to know the answers, which will severely hurt your credibility. The audience will take little or nothing back from the content of your presentation and you will look unprofessional as a presenter. By properly combining content, design, and delivery, you'll create a great presentation!

> **Mistake Proofing**
>
> ### Know More than You Show
>
> You should always be ready to answer any questions that are likely to arise. However, don't assume that the members of your audience will necessarily want or need to know all that you know. As a friend once remarked, "It's not hard to know a lot of stuff; what's hard is to know what stuff to share." But if you know why you're doing the presentation and for whom, that decision gets a lot easier.

The Process

There is a process to creating that great presentation. First, you must create your content. Then, you must design for that content. Finally, you must develop your delivery strategy and style.

Content

There are some key steps to keep in mind when creating your content. First, you do your research. Then, group the information into logical categories. Finally, you create your outline. (We'll get into that in Chapter 2.)

Too often presenters don't follow those key steps. The night before a meeting, they're cramming information onto slides trying to create this great presentation. They may even be adding items to their presentation at the last minute.

To avoid the problems of late preparation and last-minute editing, think of creating the content of your presentation in terms of these three steps:

Don't Wrap It Up CAUTION!

Some people feel that properly preparing for a presentation means putting together a package that cannot change. But we've all attended presentations that came across as canned.

Put your package together, but keep alert to any changes in the context of your presentation: new information, a shift in mood, a sense of greater interest or urgency. Don't hesitate to adjust your presentation to make it more effective by being fresh and current.

1. Do your research.
2. Group your information into logical categories.
3. Create your outline.

Design

Once you've outlined your presentation, you're ready to create your slides and add graphics, charts, and animation. Chapters 3, 4, 5, and 6 are dedicated to helping you take your presentation from outline form to a solid complete piece of work.

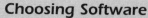

Choosing Software

Smart Managing   There are numerous presentation programs on the market, including free software. You may already have a program on your computer or your organization may use a certain program, so you don't need to choose. If you've got a choice, you can read the reviews in periodicals and on the Web. If you're unsure, it's probably wisest to go with what Gregg Keizer of (*CNET Review*, Oct. 12, 2000) called "the reigning prince of presentations ... the presentation standard"—PowerPoint.

Noting that it's "slightly pricey," he recommended for smaller budgets StarOffice Impress, which is free.

I would add that I gave a rating of 5 out of 5 to Astound Presentation (*Presentations*, November 2000), noting that it contains "pretty much everything a PowerPoint junky could ever want."

Although there are other presentation programs (such as Corel Presentations, Astound Presentation, Sun Microsystem Impress, and Lotus Freelance), in this book we discuss how to create your presentation using Microsoft PowerPoint. We show you how to create the proper slide, when to use images, and the proper way to use charts. We also offer insights into creating that great presentation.

Delivery

And finally, there's the delivery. You need to know the logistics of your meeting. (We cover that subject in Chapter 7.) You need to understand how to make the participants retain your message. (Just because you're talking and participants appear to be listening does not mean there is knowledge being transferred from you to them.) You need to set clear objectives in the presentation as well as state your expectations for your audience. They need to find value in your presentation. Your presentation needs to be such that what you present and how you present it causes a change in behavior of those who attend the presentation. Maybe it's a case of helping them to better understand the long-range vision of the company; if you can get them to see it in a way that helps them embrace change, improves morale, and increases productivity, your presentation has done the job. Chapters 8 and 9 will help you deliver that great presentation that gets results.

> ### Beware the Tyranny of Your Tools
> Don't let your software dictate the content, design, and delivery of your presentation. In his online article, "The Tyranny of Presentation Software," Rick Altman warns that presentation software "dummies" down good presenters:
>
> "In too many cases, presentation software has detracted from speeches, not enhanced them. ...
>
> "Resist. Don't fall prey to the tyranny. Don't let the presentation software take over the presentation. If you're an experienced speaker, make sure that the software doesn't turn you into a robot. If you're not experienced, don't expect the software to save you. ... Presentation software is a tool, it is not the art itself. In the hands of an artist, the tool can do wonderful things. In the wrong hands, it can turn a good speaker into a bad one, and a bad one into a dreadful one."

The Situation

Up to this point, we've been dealing with presentations in general. That may be the best way to begin a book on presentations, but it's the worst way to begin any presentation—and probably the best way to fail.

When you decide or find out that you're going to do a presentation, get all of the details. This advice might seem obvious, but some people immediately start thinking and/or worrying about what they'll do, getting at least one big step ahead of themselves before they really know where they're going.

The details that you should get will generally fall into four categories, which you can remember as the four P's:

- Purpose
- People
- Point
- Place

Purpose

Why are you doing this presentation? The full answer to that question is your purpose. And that full answer has two parts.

The first part is your subject area, the *what* of your presentation. What will you be addressing or covering? The proposed

TRICKS OF THE TRADE

Rating Presentations

Here's how Rick Altman rates presentations ("The Tyranny of Presentation Software"):

- *Best Presentation:* Truly excellent speaker, great ideas, and slides that amplify on the points made, instead of repeating them.
- *Very Good:* Truly excellent speaker, great ideas, and no slides.
- *Still OK:* Excellent speaker, redundant slides that don't add anything.
- *Not So Good:* Bad speaker, good slides.
- *Pretty Bad:* Bad speaker, no slides.
- *The Worst:* Bad speaker, redundant slides.

As you prepare a presentation, imagine your audience rating you by this scale. How would you score?

changes in the employee manual? The recent negative media reports about the new product? The update of the company intranet?

It's essential to find out how broad or narrow your scope should be and how deep you should go—aspects that depend to a great extent on the other P's. It may be just as important to find out if there's anything that you should avoid, such as a proposal that the board is still debating or a recent resignation in the department that developed the new product.

The second part of your purpose is the reason, the *why* of your presentation. What are you expected to do? Provide information? Help participants understand? Persuade them to agree on something? Motivate them to act? Entertain them? There may be several reasons for doing the presentation. Unless you know them all, it's not likely that you'll balance and structure your presentation appropriately.

The full answer to the *why* question may not come easily— or at all. Sometimes you have to ask and then ask again—and sometimes you have to figure out the rest of the answer by yourself.

Let's take an example. The CEO asks you to provide new employees with an overview of the employee manual. It may seem that your reason is simple: to inform. But there may be other reasons behind her request. She may not mention that she's concerned about low morale in the company and is hoping that you'll help the new hires understand the reasons behind certain unpopular policies. She may not mention that she suspects that the managers responsible for other aspects of the orientation program may have come across as serious and uncaring and is expecting that you'll be entertaining enough to change their image of the company.

The *why* of your purpose is probably as important as the *what*—and it often may be even more important. If it makes sense to ask, do so. If it's wiser to find out on your own, do so. You don't want to find out about hidden agendas or unexpressed expectations too late.

People

To whom are you delivering this presentation? The answer to that question may seem simple enough, especially if you know the target group. But make sure you know how much or how little they know about the subject of your presentation and why they need to know any more.

You might imagine yourself sitting among those people. Answer the following key questions:

- Why are you attending this presentation?
- How do you feel about attending it?
- What do you expect to get out of it?

If you can't imagine how those people would answer those questions, maybe you don't have a good enough sense of who they are. Find out more about them until you can answer those questions with confidence.

Point

What do you want to happen as a result of your presentation? That's the point, the objective.

How will the participants be different because of your presentation? In other words, what will be evidence that you succeeded, that you met your expectations?

If you know your purpose, why you're doing the presentation, you should have little trouble figuring out the point. (Now, as for reaching the point, well, that's where things get more complicated. . . .)

Place

Where are you doing the presentation? And don't settle for just a room designation—unless you know all about that location. Here some questions to answer:

- How big is the room?
- What is the layout of seats and other furniture? How much can it be changed, if needed?
- Where are you going to be in that room?
- What equipment will be in that room? A screen? A microphone? (What kind?) A podium?
- Where are the electrical outlets?
- Where is the connection for the intranet and/or Internet?
- How good is the lighting and how is it controlled?
- How well does the heating and air conditioning work?
- Are there windows? If so, how many, how big, and where are they? Is the view likely to distract participants? Are there curtains?
- Is the room relatively quiet? How likely is it that there will be disruptions?

You may not need to ask all of these questions, depending on the nature of your presentation. You may already have most or all of the answers. But it's always smartest to make sure.

Finally, a question that's related to location only in that it's also a logistics issue: How much time will you have for your presentation?

> **Tricks of the Trade**
>
> ### Post Your P's
> When you've got the answers to your questions about the situation for your presentation—purpose, people, point, and place—summarize them on an index card. Then, as you prepare your presentation, post that card with the four P's where you can conveniently use it as a touchstone to keep on track.

> ## Taming the Butterflies
>
> Research shows that public speaking scares many people. If you're one of them, or if you just feel nervous, you could use the technique of visualization. This may work better the more you know about the situation for your presentation—and it's definitely more effective when you prepare well.
>
> Imagine yourself beginning with confidence, making a great first impression, establishing rapport with the participants. Imagine your preparation paying off as you move through your presentation with poise, ready for anything. Choose positive, successful images of yourself and you'll feel less nervous.

Presentation Checklists

Before we move on to the chapters that get into the specifics of creating your content, designing for that content, and developing your delivery strategy and style, I think that we should start with some general guidelines for presentations. I find it helpful to use two checklists. Every time you create a presentation, I recommend that you use these checklists as guidelines for helping you to make that presentation be as effective and successful as you hope it will be.

Total Visual Checklist

The first checklist is the Total Visual Checklist. Use this one for the entire presentation. It helps you with the organization, the content, and the look of the presentation. Use this when you're reviewing your presentation as a whole.

Attribute	Description	✔
Organization		
Agenda	Present the agenda within the first three slides.	
Logical Flow	Ensure that the flow follows the agenda and is easy for the audience to follow.	
Data Clustering	Check that all information related to one topic is together.	
Account Customization	Include placeholders for account information.	

Attribute	Description	✔
Organization		
Blank or Logo Screen	Include blank or logo slides as the first and last slides of the presentation.	
Appendix	Include an appendix for easy reference for the audience.	
Hidden Slides	Use hidden slides that contain additional details; use only if needed.	
Content/Flow		
Variety	Vary the slides. For example, don't show six pie charts or six bullet slides in a row. Change slide style approximately every 3-5 slides.	
Appropriate Chart	Ensure that the type of chart you choose is the best way to display the data.	
Transitions	Build transitional phrases into your speaking notes.	
Necessity of Slide	Cut out unnecessary slides. Create hidden slides or hyperlinks to address questions that might be asked.	
Look		
Appropriate Template	Ensure that the template matches presentation objective, presentation medium, and content. Determine how best to use sidebars, titles, and footers. Determine background color: light or dark. Use best contrast: light text on dark background.	
Informative Headings	Use different headings that provide instant identification of the main point/content of slide.	
Presentation Medium	Use color, black and white, or textures in charts and graphs, based on the presentation method. For example, don't use yellow text if black and white hard copies will be left behind; yellow text can't be seen on white paper.	
Graphics	Ensure that the graphics accurately and appropriately represent the topic and message. Use appropriate graphics for your message: for a reference to something, use a symbol or clip art; for an accurate representation, use a picture or video.	

Single Visual Checklist

For each individual slide, use the Single Visual Checklist. This will help you review the organization, understanding, look, and flow for each individual slide.

Attribute	Description	✔
Organization		
Major Point	Have only one major point on each slide.	
Focal Point	Create one primary point of focus on each slide.	
Concise	Leave out information the presenter can say.	
Understanding		
Titles	Write informative titles that tell your audience the importance of the slide within three seconds.	
Illustrate	Illustrate information with charts, comparison tables, and/or pictures.	
Call Attention	Use arrows or symbols that draw attention to the important part of the chart or diagram.	
Interpretation	Build into your speaker's notes an explanation of why the data is important.	
Charts	Keep the charts simple, with a clear focus. Make sure that data points are well placed and easy to read.	
Abbreviations	Use abbreviations only when the audience will understand.	
Look		
Phrases	Use phrases; not sentences.	
Parallel Structure	Ensure that all phrases start the same way, with all verbs or all nouns.	
Limited Words	Add the fewest words needed to explain a picture or chart. Put full explanation in your speaker's notes to enable presenter to discuss.	
Fonts	Use 24-point font for text; no less than 20, if absolutely necessary. Use a sans serif type face, such as Tahoma or Arial.	
Clip Art	Use only to enhance a point; avoid cartoon clip art in most cases.	
Sizing Photos/ Clip Art	Ensure that images are sized to the appropriate scale.	
Spell Check	Check spelling of bullet points and chart information. Use software tool and check visually.	

Attribute	Description	✔
Flow		
Photographs	Ensure that there's enough memory to have photos come up quickly. Use JPEG format at a low resolution (72dpi).	
Builds	Use builds to emphasize and speak on one bullet point at a time. Choose transitions that are simple and easy on the eyes.	

Both of these checklists include information that goes beyond what is discussed in this book. So, keep these checklists handy and refer back to them often, for every presentation.

Don't worry if you don't understand all of the terms used in these checklists. We'll cover those in our discussions. I also encourage you to customize these checklists, by adding to them points that you want to remember from the chapters that follow.

Manager's Checklist for Chapter 1

❏ There are three elements to a great presentation: content, design, and delivery. *Content* includes the research and organization of materials. *Design* is the architecture of the slides and the graphical enhancements. *Delivery* is how you voice your message.

❏ Create your content in three steps: do your research, group the information into logical categories, and create your outline.

❏ Before you begin planning, know the specifics of your situation: Why are you doing this presentation? What is your subject and what is your reason? To whom are you delivering this presentation? What do you want to happen as a result of your presentation? Where are you doing the presentation? How much time will you have for your presentation?

❏ Use the Total Visual Checklist to help with the organization, the content, and the look of your presentation and the Single Visual Checklist to help with the organization, understanding, look, and flow for each individual slide.

Preparing Your Content

O nce you know what your presentation is to cover, why you're doing the presentation, and who will be attending, it's time to do some research. Research comes in many forms and goes to various levels, depending on what you know about the topic and what your participants need to know. You may have to present on a topic that you know nothing about, or it may be something that's second nature to you. You may be providing a brief overview or focusing on one aspect and going into detail.

Whatever your situation, unless this is a presentation that you give with the same information to similar audiences, you must do at least some research. You show your audience a different level of respect by researching and understanding your topic. As Ron Hoff contends in *I Can See You Naked: A Fearless Guide to Making Great Presentations* (Andrews & McMeel, 1988) "An ill-prepared presenter sends a dramatic message to his or her audience: 'I don't think you're very important. If you were, I'd be better prepared.'"

Before You Start Your Research

Before you can start your research, there are three questions you should ask yourself:

1. What do I want my audience to gain?
2. What might they already know about my topic?
3. What is the objective of the presentation?

You should already have the answers to these questions, as I pointed out in Chapter 1, under "The Situation." But now you start taking what you know about the people and the point and translating it into specifics.

For example, the purpose of your presentation may be to enable your participants to train their subordinates on a new procedure. They should already know how to train their people and they may know something about the new procedure or about the old procedure that this new procedure is replacing. The objective is to make sure that you have provided the knowledge that they need to be able to go into the field and train their people.

Asking these three questions will help you get your thoughts together about the information you'll need in this presentation. This is the "brain dump" time before you start your research. Write down whatever thoughts come to you. Don't worry about the form or the format: the thoughts that you dump don't need to be complete. They can come in the form of comments and/or questions. Write down only main points or thoughts that need more research. If in doubt, put it down. Don't worry about organizing your thoughts at this point—just dump them!

Key Term

Brain dump The act of getting out in the open everything you know about something. In terms of preparing for a presentation, the brain dump would include whatever your participants should already know about the subject, what they need to get from your presentation, how they're going to use what you present, what's likely to interest them, and what questions they might have.

This brain dump will be your research platform. Doing this brain dump prior to research will get you closer to the objective of your presentation and help you avoid boring your participants by providing too much information that they should already know.

Brain Dump Examples

There are four examples below to help you better understand the brain dump process.

For a presentation to subordinates, to review a recent sales promotion, here's a sample brain dump:

> get final financial info; match against predetermined goals and objectives; research unforeseen issues that came up, e.g., product availability issue, fulfillment issue; collect recap from direct reports, getting their feedback on the promo, e.g., issues, competitive activity, response to marketing; compare results with results from similar promo from a different time, make sure they're as similar as possible; compare vs. budget (plan) (maybe vs. last year also?); analysis on profitability, i.e., evaluating cost of promo, marketing costs; ROI; facilitate session on gathering key learning or keys to the results (takeaways), i.e., marketing investment didn't pay off, need to look more seriously at competitors' activities; when recapping financials, need to identify and document performance issues

This is a presentation to subordinates, to train them on a new procedure. Here's a sample brain dump:

> learn training materials that will be sent to team; determine some of top questions/concerns of team; be prepared to discuss change of job scope; implications of new procedure, e.g., will require additional training outside of company; manpower implications (require more or less people?)

This is a presentation to superiors, to review your subordinate's talent assessments. Here's a sample brain dump:

> need to be to the point, direct; hold meeting prior to presentation reviewing talent assessments; condense to 15-minute review; get point across and tied up; prepare for questions; need results at fingertips; be able to refer to details very quickly

This is a presentation to another company, to promote working with your organization. Here's a sample brain dump:

> get information about that company, i.e., facts about their short-comings; how can we help; learn about party presenting to; do cost comparison of us vs. known competition; show their savings when use us; establish benefits specific for them

Once you feel like you've finished your brain dump, you can start your research. This is where the who, what, when, where, why, and how come into play. (If you're not fairly sure that you've finished dumping, take a break. Come back to it later: it's a lot easier to start your research on a solid foundation than to have to add something later down the line.)

Starting Your Research

Start your research as soon as you possibly can. Give yourself the time to gather whatever content you need to prepare your presentation properly. Depending on the topic, you may need information from support teams within the company, which will require time to prepare these materials for you. Remember that some things take more time to get, especially if you have to rely on others to provide it. This is where skill in time and task management pays off.

One technique is to list all of the areas of information you need to gather, jotting down beside each the probable source(s) and the amount of time you expect it to take to get the necessary information. For example, for the fourth scenario outlined earlier, the presentation to another company, this is the list you might develop from your brain dump:

Information	Source	Time
Information about company shortcomings	newspaper archives	one hour
	Web search	half hour?
	Jane (former employee)	one hour?
	other former employees?	??
	report to shareholders	two hours

Information	Source	Time
How we can help (strengths in weak areas)	Ted (Marketing)	one day
People to attend presentation	their company executive assistant	15 minutes
Cost comparison of us vs. known competition	Pat (Accounting)	one day
Benefits specific for them	Ted (Marketing)	one day

This list is for your use only, so it may be rough or detailed, as long as it helps you plan your research. One of the basic rules of time management is to get others working first, so you get the tasks going on in parallel rather than in serial. There may also be schedule conflicts that cause delays. In this example, you'd want to talk with Ted and Pat as soon as possible and call Jane to arrange a meeting. You also need to determine which tasks depend on the results of other tasks. In this example, since the presentation is based on the shortcomings of the target company, that's where you'd need to start, before you can gather information on the complementary strengths of your organization. But you might want to call the executive assistant first to find out who would be attending your presentation, since that might give you insights into the areas where company execs are feeling vulnerable and in need of working with your organization. Finally, you should usually deal with your questions first. In our example, that would include the report to shareholders (where can you get a copy?) and talking with other former employees (can your neighbor Jane help you contact others?). It could also include searching the newspaper archives and the Web, because you may find something that you'd have to check to corroborate.

Managing Your Information

While researching your topic, you'll come across different types of information. Some of it you'll use only to better understand your subject area or the people to whom you're delivering the presentation. The rest you'll want to provide in your presentation. But it's not all of equal importance.

You should be able to put the information you want to use into two categories, need-to-know and nice-to-know. The need-to-know information is what your audience needs to know to meet the objective of your presentation. The nice-to-know information is bits that are not crucial to the objective, but may increase interest in your presentation.

Here's an example. Your company helps other companies upgrade their back-office software. You've identified this company as a prospect for an upgrade, so you're researching it to prepare for a pitch next week. As you gather information on the company, you divide it into two columns on your list.

Need-to-Know	Nice-to-Know
They need to upgrade their back-office software.	Their company was founded in 1993.
HR currently runs software.	They doubled their profits from last year.
They're jumping from version 6.0 to 8.0.	They'd rather outsource than try to do it themselves (info from an insider).

The need-to-know information belongs in your presentation, of course, and most of it also belongs on the slides. You want your audience to see as well as hear this information so they remember it better. In our scenario, the need-to-know information on this part of your list would be on the "problem" slide. This is the slide that will recap the company's situation with its back-office software. The nice-to-know information can become part of your speech script. Referring to the date their company was founded may give you some credibility for understanding their needs. The doubled profits information can allow you to talk to the reason why they need to upgrade. Knowing that they would rather outsource allows you a transition, such as "John

> ## Never Burn a Source
> If you've gotten information from an insider, respect that person's right to confidentiality. Don't reveal the identity of your source unless you've gotten permission from him or her in advance to do so. (That's what journalists call "burning a source" and it's considered a major violation of faith.) If you don't have permission to cite your source for something you know, use what you know but introduce it otherwise: "I would assume that ..." or "You've certainly considered the advantages of ..." or "It would make sense, given the history and culture of your company, that ...."

here says you would prefer to outsource this upgrade and here's how we can help."

You may also have some statistics that are not crucial to your presentation, but that you want to keep handy, to share verbally, depending on how your audience is reacting to your presentation. Other forms of nice-to-know information can be answers to handle questions, pushback, or concerns from your audience.

Try to anticipate these and be prepared to discuss all different personal agendas from the audience. Perhaps the best way is to imagine yourself in the shoes of each of the participants or of typical participants. What do you want to know? How do you feel about the context of the presentation, about your

> **Pushback** Any negative reaction, including questions, objections, and resistance. A good presenter understands that this is usually normal give-and-take, even a sign of connecting with the audience and being open to interaction. A presenter who's prepared properly can handle most pushback ... maybe even welcome it.

need to be there? What do you think of the presentation? Has it met your expectations? What questions do you have? What concerns do you want to express?

If you know about the people who will be attending your presentation, you should be able to anticipate their reactions. If you can anticipate their reactions, you should be able to prepare for them.

Keep Your Audience in Mind

Knowing your audience will also help you separate your information into need-to-know and nice-to-know. Always make sure you're familiar with your audience before you separate your information. Otherwise, your presentation will likely come across as a one-size-fits-all package.

For instance, if you're giving a project update to the Senior Team, detailed information becomes nice-to-know. This is information you should know and be prepared to talk about, but not necessarily have on slides. They do not want to sit through a 60-slide, heavy text presentation. For this audience, the need-to-know information is simple and to the point. On the other hand, if you're giving the same presentation to the engineers, then your approach to the information changes. Because the engineers will want to know the details, those specifics that don't interest the Senior Team now become the need-to-know information and you use a different format. As you can see, your objective (to update on the project) and your message (progress, problems, etc.) should not change, but only the way you choose and present the information.

Researching a Known Topic

Researching for a presentation when you already know a lot about the topic is different from researching an area unfamiliar to you. Here's an example of how you would research for a topic you're already familiar with.

Let's say you're giving another sales pitch to a new prospect. You know your company information inside and out, but what do you know about the prospect and why do they need what you're offering?

You know what it's like when someone comes in to meet with you and your co-workers and tries to talk to you like he or she knows your company and its problems. Most of the time, the presentation comes across as weak, as a canned, generic presentation.

You know that those presentations are generally not very effective and they can undermine the credibility of the person doing the presentation. If you want to deliver an effective pitch and really connect with a prospect, you have to focus the presentation on them—their company, their situation, their problems, and their needs.

Make sure you know your facts about your client and how your product or services will help them. If you don't have a good understanding of what they do and their needs, then you don't belong there—yet. If you don't have a contact who can provide information, then usually a company's Web site is the best place to start your research. Also, try to get some of their printed materials. When you read it, pay attention not only to the words and images but also to the order and structure of what's there—and to what's not there. (As a friend of mine would remind me, "The forgotten art of writing is knowing what to leave out.") As you gather information, don't neglect the small stuff. It's often useful to weave trivia about the prospect into your presentation.

For an external audience, it's best either to tell a story so the participants can more easily follow the message or to use a problem/solution approach, so keep this in mind when doing your research. You might, for example, find out about a valued customer that recently left your prospect for a competitor because your prospect didn't offer customer service through its Web site. That might make an effective story to illustrate your message. Or you might get some information from the annual report showing that sales declined last year, although the company opened two new branches, and you hear through the grapevine that your prospect's computer system can't keep up with the volume of orders. So now you've got the ingredients for a problem/solution approach that should grab their interest and hold it.

Researching an Unknown Topic

Let's say your company is rolling out a new product and you're responsible for educating your subordinates. You know nothing about this product, so you need to research it from every aspect. You must be able to talk about the features, benefits, disadvantages, sales goals, best ways to promote the product, etc. This means you have to research lots of information in a short period of time: you have to become an expert.

There are some fundamental problems or concerns in creating a presentation when you don't much if anything at all about the subject. Usually you ask yourself questions like "How can I acquire the proper information?" and "What if there's technical information that I cannot comprehend or learn in a short time?"

Use your company's resources. Someone else there has to know everything about this new product, so find the expert and interview him or her. It could be that you need to tap several "partial experts"—someone from R&D, someone from Marketing, someone from Customer Service, and so on—to put together the whole picture. Ask your experts the who, what, when, where, how, and why questions. Maybe even bring them into the meeting to present a small portion of the presentation. (Make sure, of course, that they're able to present the essential information in a way that normal people can understand. Otherwise, the strategy of using experts is likely to backfire.) Or you can invite them to serve as a test audience for a "dress rehearsal." (Bear in mind, however, that your experts will be able to comment on the accuracy of the facts in your presentation but not necessarily on your organization, style, and other elements that can mean success or failure.) Find others in the company who can help you with the data, such as past years' performance of other products, sales goals, projected growth, etc. The key is to be smart and use all of the resources around you to research your topic.

Going from Learning to Presenting

Converting what you've just learned into a presentation for your people can be a little difficult. Let's say you've just been briefed on a high-level presentation. Now, you need to turn around and create a lower-level presentation from what you've just learned. Before you begin, ask yourself these two questions:

1. What role do my people play in meeting the objectives of this presentation?

2. How will the objectives I set for them be different than the objectives set for me?

By answering these two questions, you should come up with the objectives for your presentation. Make sure you clearly define these objectives so they will lead to achieving the ultimate goal. The important thing is to set new objectives and create a presentation focused on your audience. You can't simply regurgitate the information from the high-level presentation you attended.

Converting Your Research into an Outline

Once you've completed all of your research, your next step is to organize it into an outline. Many people react negatively to the thought of making outlines, in large part because of bad experiences with the complicated schemes taught in grade school (all those Roman numerals, Arabic numbers, and capital and small letters!). But an outline is just a logical ordering of steps.

There are three steps to creating an outline:

1. Determine the outline style.
2. Group your raw data.
3. Arrange into outline format.

> ### Do It Right—from the Start
> **Smart Managing**
>
> We're all familiar with some version of the quote, "Those who fail to plan plan to fail." That's true for presentations. Sure, you may not really fail if you don't plan, but your presentation won't be as effective without planning—and it may take more time and energy if you don't have a good plan.

Determine the Outline Style

Before creating your outline, you need to determine the type of outline style. Here are three main types of outline styles that we may use on a day-to-day basis and four others that may also be appropriate:

- **Chronological**—shows events in order as they occurred
- **Narrative** (story telling)—takes the audience on a journey through a flowing presentation

- **Problem/solution**—states the problem, the why's, your solution, and a summary
- **Cause/effect**—states the cause and explains the effect(s)
- **Topical**—divides the general topic into several subtopics
- **Journalistic questions**—uses some or all of the what, who, where, when, why, and how questions
- **Spatial**—follows a linear logic based on location, direction, and space

You should choose your outline style according to your subject, the group attending your presentation, and the time allowed. You may want to try several styles to outline your presentation, to determine which seems best. It may take a little longer, but it's worth the extra time to get the most appropriate style. (Don't worry about Roman numerals, Arabic numbers, and capital and small letters. Format your points and subpoints in whatever way makes the most sense to you. After all, you're going to be using your outline, not submitting it for a grade or for publication!)

First, list the main points that you want to make in your presentation, following the logic of your outline style—chronological, narrative, problem/solution, cause/effect, topical, journalistic questions, or spatial. Some guides recommend three to five main points, but you should make your decision based on your subject, the group, and the time. (One "fact" of presenting that's been cited for a while is that most people attending a presentation will remember no more than five key points. Some claim that three is the max.)

Then, list under each main point the subpoints, again following the chosen outline style. You may want to break down the subpoints further, if it helps you to do so. (I don't worry about any "rules" for outlines; do what works for you and your particular situation.)

Generally, there are three parts to an outline: introduction, body, and conclusion. Each of these three parts of your outline will be different, depending on the type of presentation you're

Sample Outline

Here's a simple outline for a presentation on promoting a new product.

Introduction
1. The product
2. The market situation

Possible strategies
1. Television ads
2. Radio ads
3. Newspaper ads
4. Direct mail marketing
5. Web
6. Combination of strategies

Recent promotional campaigns and results
1. Our company
2. Our competitors

Analysis of each strategy
1. Cost
2. Effectiveness
3. Disadvantages

Conclusion and recommendations

giving and the group attending it. The body will consist of your main points and all of your subpoints. That should be your focus now. You may already have some great ideas for the introduction and/or the conclusion even before you flesh out your outline. If so, great! If not, don't worry: you'll likely be inspired as you prepare your outline and organize your information.

Finally, read through your outline as if you were one of the people who'll be attending your presentation. Does the organization seem to proceed point by point in a way that will be easiest to understand and will be most effective? Experienced speakers quite often revise an outline several times before moving on to the next step.

Group Your Raw Data

Once you've finalized your outline, you're ready to cluster your information, so you can attach all of the pieces of your research results to your outline. Start by grouping similar pieces of infor-

Sticky Notes

Here's an easy way to make sure you get your outline in proper order. Write each of your main concepts onto a sticky note. Then, take the sticky notes and make piles that belong together. It's easier to create order out of your data because you're physically grouping the pieces into piles. Also, it's easier to move the notes around.

mation from your research into "clusters." For instance, put all company information in one cluster, client information into another, product information into another, and so forth.

Once you have your clusters, create a logical order of the information within each cluster: put each main point first, then any supporting information. Do this for each of your clusters of information.

Arrange into Outline Format

Now that you've formed clusters of your information, you can insert your clusters into their proper place in the outline. If you've organized your outline appropriately, this step should be relatively easy. The body will be the bulk of the presentation. It will consist of your main points, subpoints, and the information needed to make your points and subpoints.

After you've put together the pieces of the body, you should be ready to do the introduction and the conclusion.

What might be in your introduction? It should set the stage for the rest of the presentation. This means it should include an agenda and clarify the goals and objective of your presentation. The introduction can include an overview of a situation, a statement of the current situation of the organization, or a recap of history. During this time, you want to grab the attention of your participants, by appealing to their interests and/or goals or creating a point of reference that's important to them. Your introduction should fit your outline style. For a chronological outline, set the timeline. If it's narrative, set the stage for the story you're telling. If it's problem/solution, uncover the problem. For a cause/effect approach, describe the cause. If your style is topical, mention your main topic and list your subtopics. If you're using journalistic questions to structure your presentation, you can simply ask the questions or you can also provide short answers and promise to elaborate. If your approach is spatial, you might describe the general area you'll be covering, perhaps citing some of the specific stops along your journey.

Be creative. In the introduction to your speech, you want to get the attention of your participants and then focus their attention on what you'll be doing. You also want to make a connection with your audience and establish your credibility. You might try opening with a quote, a question, humor (risky!), a creative image, an anecdote, or a sharing of emotions.

One word of advice: be careful not to put too much information in the front of the presentation. When we're very familiar with a topic, we tend to provide too much information. Don't go with what you know. Go instead with what your audience needs and wants to know. A presentation isn't just about providing information; it's about making effective use of that information.

The WIIFM "Ruler"

We've all heard about WII-FM—not a radio station, but "What's in it for me?" That's the question on most people's minds when you start your presentation. Since that question rules their minds, it should serve as the ruler by which you measure your introduction. Imagine that you're somebody in the front row asking, "What's in it for me?" after every sentence. How long does it take to get the answer?

Take Humor Seriously

Humor can do a lot to build rapport—especially if you direct your humor toward yourself—and to keep your audience interested and attentive. But it can also hurt your presentation. Tell appropriate jokes only—and only when appropriate, either to help make a point or to mark a break between sections. And remember these four points:

• Some people just can't tell jokes.
• Some groups are tough crowds.
• Some topics just aren't suitable for humor.
• Many jokes really aren't all that funny.

> **Tricks of the Trade**
>
> ## Tell, Tell, Tell
>
> The classic advice for presenters and writers is the "three tell" rule:
> - Tell them what you're *going to tell* them.
> - Tell them what you *want to tell* them.
> - Then tell them what you *told* them.
>
> As long as human nature stays the same, that advice just makes good sense.

The conclusion should summarize the main points of your presentation, provide closure, and leave an impression. The conclusion can consist of recommendations, questions, future directions, next steps to take, goals and objectives, timelines, and so forth. For chronological presentations, it ends the sequence and tells of next steps. For problem/solution, it should recap the benefits, get buy-in, and discuss timelines.

To help make your conclusion more memorable, you might consider using any of the strategies that help an introduction get attention: a quote, a question, humor, a creative image, an anecdote, or a sharing of emotions.

> **Tricks of the Trade**
>
> ## First and Last Steps in Your Journey
>
> The most important words in your presentation are your first statement and your last. That's what most people will remember best. Craft those two statements carefully. Open with a statement that will get their attention. Close with a statement that will cause them to feel and/or to take action.

Writing Your Script

After you've created your outline, it's time to design your script. Because of the steps you've taken to get this far, you should have a good idea of what you want to say and how you want to say it. This should make your script writing very easy.

Because you're so familiar with your topic, your script can be very loose. It may even be more of an outline rather than a true script. Start with the information on the slide and then integrate your notes into your script. You can also add analogies and examples in your script to help your audience better understand the meaning.

It's also important to use proper transition phrases in your script. These will help you guide your audience. The simplest would be statements such as "That brings us to my next point, which is ..."

> **Transition phrase** A sentence or two that helps move your audience from the information on your current slide to the information on the new slide by drawing attention to the relationship between them.

and "Finally, we should consider ...." Better transitions make more explicit connections: "Now that we've covered the features of our new product, we're ready to turn to strategies for promoting it" or "Following this brief discussion of widgets, let's move on to the second product line, thingamajigs."

Try to always speak in positives. Emphasize what *to do* rather than what *not to do*.

Finally, remember to keep to the time you've dedicated per point and per slide. It's very easy to stray from your plans when you're writing your script. That's the secret to developing a two-hour presentation for a 45-minute time slot.

Guidelines

Now, you should have all the information you need to create a great presentation. Before we can move to converting your content into a presentation, make sure you follow these guidelines in this chapter. Here's a quick list of questions to help you:

- Did you give yourself enough time to do the research?

> **Using PowerPoint's AutoContent Wizard**
>
> If you're having trouble trying to determine how to organize your presentation, try using the AutoContent Wizard in PowerPoint. Go to File>New and select the Presentation tab. The first icon should be the AutoContent Wizard. Single-click the wizard and click OK. First, select the presentation type. Then, answer the rest of the wizard's questions and the presentation is completed for you. All you have to do is go through the slides and fill in the recommended information.

- Did you start with the brain dump?
- Did you separate your information between need-to-know and nice-to-know?
- Did you create your outline for your audience?
- Did you use the proper outline style?
- Did you write your script?

Manager's Checklist for Chapter 2

❑ Start your research by answering three questions:
1. What do I want my audience to gain?
2. What might they already know about my topic?
3. What is the objective of the presentation?

❑ As you gather information, divide what you want to use into two categories, need-to-know (crucial to the objective of your presentation) and nice-to-know (useful for increasing interest or dealing with pushback).

❑ Determine the style for your outline depending on the nature of your presentation, then develop the outline in keeping with that style.

❑ Cluster your pieces of information and insert them as appropriate in the outline.

❑ Develop an introduction that gets and focuses attention, makes a connection, and establishes your credibility and a conclusion that summarizes the main points, provides closure, and leaves an impression.

Converting the Content into a Slide Presentation

Now that you have your content organized and in outline form, it's time to convert it into a presentation. This is probably one of the hardest steps and most often omitted or neglected. Presenters may just put their outline directly into a presentation, without taking any time to pull out the proper information and create bullet points from the outline's main points.

By just converting your outline into a presentation, you're preparing for disaster. You won't engage the participants because you'll be reading from the slides and you'll lose them very quickly because they'll be overwhelmed by the amount of information on the slides.

From Outline to Bullets

Reduce your outline to the essentials your audience needs to know for you to reach your objective. Make your point as you speak—don't put the whole point on the slide. Ask yourself, "Will putting this information on the slide help me reach my objective of this presentation?"

Here are some key rules to follow when creating bulleted text:

- Use one concept per slide.
- Use key words and phrases (noun and verbs).
- Stay within the 8 x 8 rule.
- Make your bullet points consistent in structure.
- Capitalize properly.

Use One Concept per Slide

You need to spoon-feed your audience the information. Just like a baby won't accept more than one spoonful of food at a time, your audience will not accept more than one concept per slide.

Here's an example. We may want to cross-reference or show the relationship between some information and we put it all on one slide (Figure 3-1). This can be overwhelming.

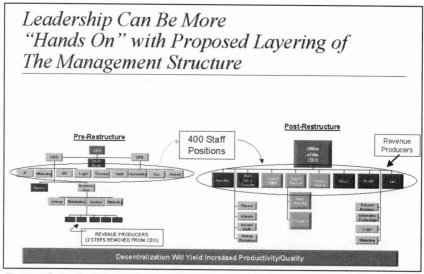

Figure 3-1. A slide with too many concepts

We should spread out this information over two or several slides, so we can walk the audience through the thought process of the cross-reference (Figure 3-2). Remember: feed them with a spoon, not a bulldozer.

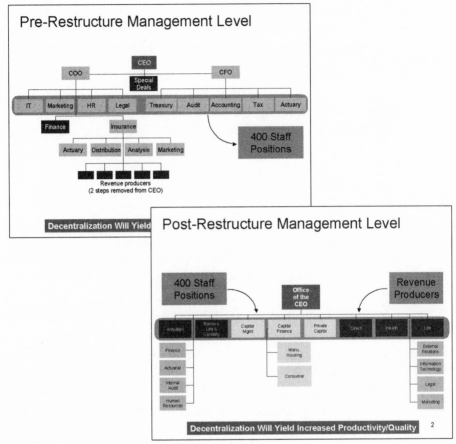

Figure 3-2. Spreading information over more than one slide

Use Key Words and Phrases

To create bullets from your outline, use key words and phrases, primarily nouns and verbs. If you put just the essentials on your slides, you'll engage your participants: they'll want to know more about these key words and phrases. So, once again, the focus is on you, not your slides. If you recreate your script word-for-word on your slides, participants will stop listening to you. Also, long sentences take participants longer to read and absorb.

Another argument for the minimalist approach: the more words you use, the harder it is to fit the text onto your slides.

(We'll get to the question of font sizes in Chapter 5.) And it's a waste of time.

Here are some keys to creating your bullet points from the outline:

- Be as concise as possible.
- Use action words or verbs.
- Delete non-impact words such as "while," "that," and "but."
- Do not use intensifying adverbs such as "really" and "very."

Stay Within the 8 x 8 Rule

What is the 8 x 8 rule? The 8 x 8 rule helps us not to overwhelm our audience with too much information and it should ensure that all the members of your audience can view and read the text.

The rule is to have no more than eight lines of text per slide and no more than eight words per line. You should be able to stick to this simple rule if you use only key words or phrases.

It's possible to stretch this rule a little, depending on the font you use. For instance, you may be able to get 12 words per line if you use a condensed font, like Arial Condensed. But it's best not to find ways to get around this rule.

Try sticking to the 8 x 8 rule when converting your outline to bulleted text. This will ensure that your text is big enough for all participants to read, even from the back of the room. Applying this rule will also help the spoon-feeding process.

Make Your Bullet Points Consistent in Structure

It's important to start your bullet points with either a noun or verb and put them in the same tense (past, present, future) and voice (active or passive). This parallel structure will help your audience understand your point more quickly.

Here's an example. Compare these two sets of bullets in terms of ease of reading and impact.

- Created several outlines
- Review of the topic
- The theme will be sold

versus

- Create several outlines
- Review the topic
- Sell the theme

Most people would consider the second set of bullets to be easier to read and to have greater impact, because of their parallel sentence structure.

Using parallel sentence structure helps your audience read through your bullet points quicker. It also helps you create bullets that are more concise and to the point.

Capitalize Properly

Capitalization is a very controversial topic. Can I use all capital letters? Should I capitalize the first letter of every word? Do I capitalize at all?

Here's the key. Adults have subconsciously memorized the shape of lowercase words, as in reading a book, a newspaper, or a magazine. So, if you put your text in all capital letters, it takes them longer to make words out of the groups of letters and phases out of the groups of words. If you capitalize the first letter of every word, they have to stop and read each word separately, then go back and comprehend the meaning of the phrase as a whole. When you capitalize the first letter of the first word only, they see it as a whole and can understand it faster.

We're used to reading text in sentence format. Remember this when creating your bullets. Treat each bullet point as a sentence without punctuation. Capitalize only the first letter of the first word and any proper nouns in your bullet points. This is called *sentence case*. For the titles of your slides, it is acceptable to capitalize the first letter of every word. This is called *title case*. This will draw more attention to the titles of your slides, so participants take a little more time to read the titles, which puts

How to Quickly Change the Case

If you already have your presentation done and you need to change the case of the text, PowerPoint gives you a quick way to format the text. First, select your text, then go to Format>Change Case. The Change Case pop-up window appears. Your options are sentence case, lowercase, uppercase, title case, and toggle case. Select the radial button next to the format you want, then click OK.

a little more emphasis on the new information you're about to discuss. But avoid using all caps: text that's all uppercase is harder to read.

Enhancing Your Bullets

Your presentation flows logically and your bullet points are complete. Now you're ready to add some extra elements that will help present your message more effectively. But first, you need to determine the right amount and type of slides. Then you can decide how to grab attention and how to make sure participants understand the information in your presentation.

Determine the Number of Slides

If you have a certain amount of time allotted for your presentation, you must start backward. No matter how much information you have in your outline, you can present only so much information in the time allowed. The general rule is one or two slides per minute. So, if you have 15 minutes in front of the VP, your presentation should be no longer than 30 slides.

But you must also keep your audience in mind when trying determining the approximate number of slides to use. A VP probably doesn't want to sit through a 30-slide presentation. You should have more condensed and top-level information in the presentation, so it takes you longer to present each slide.

You must also in mind your style as a presenter. Do you elaborate too much on information? Are you a "talker"? Or are you to the point with your information? If you're a "talker," then you want fewer slides, in order to keep your presentation to the time allotted. If you can be brief and to the point, then it's OK to

---

Know Yourself

Smart Managing

On the walls of the ancient temple of Apollo at Delphi was inscribed the imperative, "Know yourself." This old Greek maxim makes sense thousands of years later. How do you deliver presentations? What is your speaking speed? Do you stick to your script or do you elaborate? In practical terms, how many slides should you use in a 30-minute presentation?

You should be able to answer that last question at least before you can determine the number of slides to prepare. As you rehearse and present, you'll develop a good idea of how many slides to include in a presentation, varying it somewhat according to the material and the audience.

---

have more slides, because you will go through them more quickly.

Create Proper Titles

The title should be the main point of your slide. This is the key concept that you will elaborate on in the slide's bullets. Informative titles use action verbs. If you use a noun title, include a subtitle that states the main point. This works especially well with charts and graphs. For product titles, use an action subtitle.

For each audience, review your whole presentation, then write titles based on that audience's specific interests.

Before and After

For Example

Required Elements For Assessing Cost-Effectiveness
- Explicitly understand the perspective of the cost-effectiveness analysis
- Identify the potential benefits of the technique, program, or procedure being evaluated
- Understand the type and method for determining "cost"

This text is wordy and difficult to read. We revised it as follows:

Required Elements
- Understand the perspective of the cost-effectiveness analysis
- Identify the potential benefits of the technique, program, or procedure
- Determine the type and method for "cost"

For instance, if you're speaking to higher-up management and this is a presentation about your sales results, use titles such as "Goals we reached" and "Increased profits by 50%." These titles will grab their attention.

Hook Your Audience

Set the tone of the presentation by using a "hook phrase." Use phrases such as "How would you like to improve your profits by 50%?" This will grab their attention and set the stage for the presentation.

To create powerful hooks, you must determine key measures of success for your audience—a client, a subordinate, your boss, etc.—that will get their attention: e.g., increase revenue, decrease cost, save 4K per month, increase productivity, etc. You don't have to limit your use of these hook phrases to the opening of your presentation. You can use them throughout the presentation. But be careful that your hooks don't come across as too crass, such as "What's it going to take to get you into this unit?"

The important thing to remember is to be able to back up your "promises" with data and facts. Intangible or emotional phrases—e.g., improve moral or increase satisfaction—are a little more difficult to back up.

Your hook phrases may also promise a "benefit" that your audience has not identified as a need. So, throughout the presentation, you must convince them that there's a need and show them the benefit to back it up. You must make sure that you can show this benefit in many ways throughout the presentation so the entire audience will understand. Remember: don't over-promise and under-deliver!

Ensure Transfer of Knowledge

Your participants will not all learn and think alike. That's why it's important to feed them information in different formats throughout the presentation. One format may be in bullet points. Another might be in the form of a comparison chart. Still another format might be financial data. You may have a series of three slides that tell the same story, but in a different way.

This will ensure that all members of your audience will grasp the information because you've displayed it in a format that works for them. Make sure that you're creating your slides to transfer knowledge to everyone in the audience. (See Chapter 8 for more on transferring knowledge.)

Agenda and Recap Slides

You should always have an *agenda slide* and a *recap slide* in every presentation. This practice follows the classic advice quoted in Chapter 2: "Tell them what you're *going to tell* them. Tell them what you *want to tell* them. Then tell them what you *told* them."

The agenda slide will help set the stage for the entire presentation. It will let your audience know exactly what will be discussed or learned in today's meeting.

The recap slide is just as important. Its purpose is to remind the audience what they should be taking away from the meeting, summarize your message, or make a call to action. It will also let you know if you've met the objectives of the presentation as set in your agenda slide.

Agenda slide A slide that lists the main points of a presentation. In PowerPoint an agenda slide consists of a simple list of hyperlinked topics, each linked to a group of slides, called a *custom show*. Clicking an item on the agenda slide runs the custom show and then automatically returns to the agenda slide.

Recap slide A slide that restates the main points of a presentation.

Transition Using Title Slides

It's important to transition your audience from one agenda topic to another. Use title slides for this transition, to prepare your participants to get into a different mindset for the information they're about to hear from you. These slides are pulled directly from your agenda slide. For example, if your agenda slide says, "Overview, Products, Services, and Future," then your presentation should have four title slides with the same exact titles at the beginning of each of these four sections. Figure 3-3 shows an agenda slide and the first of five title slides stemming from the agenda.

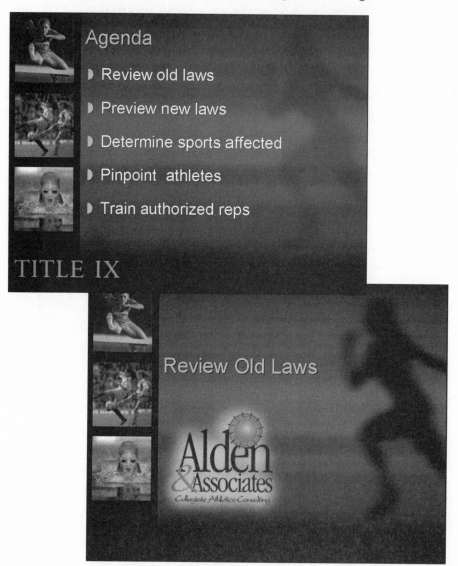

Figure 3-3. An agenda slide and a title slide

Blank Slides

Think about where in your presentation you should add blank or placeholder slides. To be effective, these slides should remain blank or have little text. They can be more graphic and can be formatted from the title slide in your master. (See Chapter 4 for guidance on setting up your masters.)

There are several uses for these slides:

- Breaks or lunch
- Whiteboard or flip chart breakouts
- Moments in your presentation when you want to audience to focus on you

Getting Rid of Bullets

After you've created your bullets, take your presentation one step further. Go back through your slides and determine where you can replace bullets or provide some relief.

Generally, you want to change the layout of the information on the slides every three to five slides. This means if you have a text-heavy presentation, approximately every three to five slides add a graphic or chart. Don't force these slides into the presentation; add them only if it makes sense. Don't add a "screen bean" character from the clip art gallery every three to five slides just to follow the guidelines. Add professional-looking imagery and charts where it makes sense and will help to emphasize or detail the main point of the slide.

PowerPoint Slide Layouts

There are 24 types of slide layouts in PowerPoint. Only one of these is for a slide with bulleted text. Use the other layouts to help you get rid of the simple bullet point slide. When you insert a new slide (Insert>New Slide), it brings up the New Slide layout pop-up window. If you single-click on any one of the layouts, in the bottom right corner it will tell you the type of slide layout. For instance, you may want to put a little text on the left of the slide and an image on the right. For this, you would use the "Text & ClipArt" layout. Try using different layout types to liven up your presentation and provide relief from bulleted slides.

How to Handle Quotes

If you must add a quote to your presentation, make sure it's short and to the point. These may be customer testimonials or information for your VP that you feel will add value to the presentation. If the quote is more than two sentences, shorten it. First, try to get the person being quoted to shorten the quote. If this is not possible, condense it to no more than two sentences, keeping the key message intact. Again, use key words and phrases. Keep only the important phrases and insert ellipses (...) to indicate that words were dropped from the quote. This way, you don't risk overwhelming the audience with a full slide paragraph of text and you can elaborate on the quote.

Adding Questions to Your Presentation

Reading a question on paper is different from reading it on the screen. It can have more impact and you can use it in various ways.

Bulleting questions on a slide makes it easier for the audience to read and comprehend the questions. It also allows for you to interact more with the audience, because you don't have to read the slide to them.

For instance, take a question that has three parts—"How do we increase revenue, enhance productivity, and establish measures?"—and convert it into bullet points and you fill in the gaps when you deliver the presentation. The title could read, "How do we ...". The bullets would read, "increase revenue?," "enhance productivity?," and "establish measures?" Posing the questions on a slide this way would allow the focus to still remain on you while getting the participants to think about the answer.

Using Graphics

We're going to discuss graphics later in this book. But they should be mentioned here, at least in passing, because of their importance in replacing or enhancing bullet text.

Making Data into Charts and Tables

If you want your audience to really see your point, express it in a chart or a table. Graphics can represent information more concisely than bullet points and help your audience to see the relationship of the data. Charts are especially good to use in technical presentations.

The key is to construct the chart to make sure participants see the data as you want them to interpret it. For instance, if you want them to see the major increase in sales over the past three years, you probably don't want to plot the past 36 months in one chart. This may show a steady increase, but not the major jump that you're trying to show them. So, plot only every six months or just each of the three years. Also, make sure that you group your data into logical categories and then put it into a logical order for presenting (Figure 3-4). (See Chapter 6 for more on charts.)

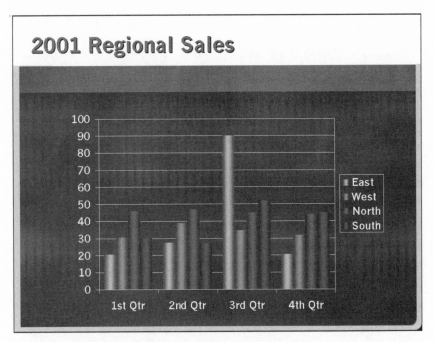

Figure 3-4. Grouping data into logical categories

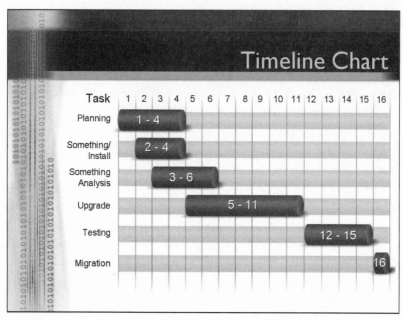

Figure 3-5. A chart that helps organize information for presenting

Charts and tables are excellent to use when you're comparing data. They help your audience see the comparisons in the information. They also help you to logically organize the information for presenting, as in the chart in Figure 3-5.

So, instead of using bullet points to list all the pieces of information, use a table to graphically compare those pieces. Basically, by using charts and tables, you're once again spoonfeeding the raw data to the audience by making it easier to take in and process.

⚠️ CAUTION!   **Beware of the Power**

Charts and tables can be far more powerful than bullets, for better or for worse. If you choose your design according to your information and your objective and structure it appropriately, your charts and tables can be very effective. On the other hand, if not, your design may obfuscate or even distort your information. Then you risk distracting or even confusing participants as they try to figure out the meaning of your graphic.

Adding Graphics to Emphasize Bullets

A graphic is worth a thousand words. This "ancient proverb" is perhaps even truer now than when an advertising agent created it in the 1920s.

Considering the potential impact of graphics and the ease of using them with presentation software, it makes sense to add some to your presentation. Graphics come in the form of symbols, clip art, photos, and video. Go through your presentation and see where you can logically add a graphic to help make your point. Adding graphics will increase the attention of the audience and it will also help participants retain your points and the content. Also, adding graphics will help you keep to the guideline of changing the layout of the slides every three to five slides, as shown in the examples in Figures 3-6 and 3-7. (Chapter 6, Adding Pizzazz, covers graphics in greater detail.)

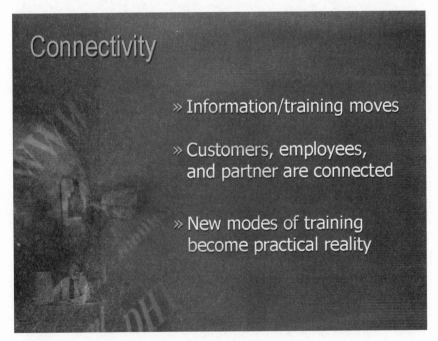

Figure 3-6. Adding graphics to keep slides fresh

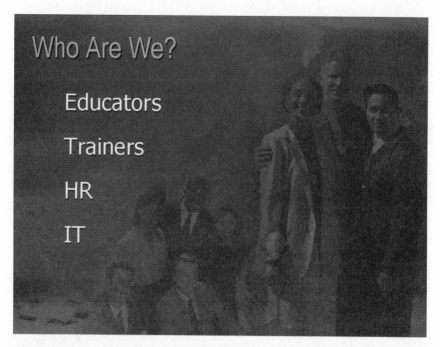

Figure 3-7. Another example of adding a graphic to a slide

Presentation Handouts

Handouts are one of the most underused tools for ensuring retention of presentation content. Most presenters feel an obligation to provide tangible takeaways. The good news is that PowerPoint makes it easy to print presentations. The bad news is ... that PowerPoint makes it easy to print presentations. As a result, most presenters just print out their presentation in black and white and give it to their audience.

That's not really a problem. But if you just print your presentation, you're throwing away a great opportunity.

Here's what happens. Participants "forget" approximately 90% of everything you said within 24 hours. This "forgotten" information is actually put into the long-term memory. That's why a good handout is so important. It will help your audience remember.

Since your handout is equally as important as your presentation, you should co-create them. When you're researching your topic, you come across information that you decide not to put onto your slides. You may use these nuggets in your script—or you may just leave them out.

You should add this information to your handouts, along with the key points of the slides. Doing this helps you to be and appear more knowledgeable about your material. You can also add resources that you come across in your research, such as Web sites, magazine articles, company materials such as white papers, and case studies. These resources add value for participants who want to know more about a specific part of your presentation.

It's OK to include the thumbnails of your slides in the handout, because they serve as a visual reminder of how the content was organized and presented. When you include the slides, you help the participants retain the information they're learning about that particular slide.

A Quick Way to Create Great Handouts

Tricks of the Trade

PowerPoint offers several styles of handouts. Here's how you can easily make handouts that participants will keep and use.

Put all of your elaboration of your key points and those additional nuggets in the Notes Page (View>Notes Page). The Notes Page will be preformatted in a bullet style, but you can change it to sentence format, which may make it easier to add full pieces of information. Add this elaboration of the slides to the Notes Page simultaneously as you create your slides.

Then, once you've finished and saved the presentation, go to File>Send To>Microsoft Word. This will bring up a pop-up menu where you choose the handout layout. Select the top layout—Notes Next to Slides—and click OK to copy your slides and notes into a Word document that you can use for your handout. You can also click the Paste Link radial button at the bottom of the pop-up window so that any change you make to your PowerPoint presentation will be reflected in this Word document handout. By creating your handouts this way, you give your audience more of a reference guide as a tangible takeaway.

Tips on Printing Your Slides in PowerPoint

If you need to print out your slides and you want to avoid wasting toner, here's your option. Go to File>Print and the Print pop-up window appears. At the bottom of the window, click the box next to Pure black & white. This will print your slides without the background. You'll get only the text and images that are part of the foreground.

Guidelines

By now, you should have your outline converted into proper presentation format. Here's a quick list of questions to make sure you followed the guidelines in this chapter:

• Do you have only one concept per slide?
• Did you follow the 8 x 8 rule?
• Did you use only key words and phrases?
• Are you using parallel sentence structure in your bullets?
• Are you using proper capitalization?
• Are your titles compelling?
• Do you have agenda and recap slides?
• Did you properly create and format your handouts?

Manager's Checklist for Chapter 3

❏ When creating bulleted text, use one concept per slide, use key words and phrases (noun and verbs), put no more than eight lines of text per slide and no more than eight words per line, make your bullet points consistent in structure, and capitalize properly.

❏ Determine how many slides to use in your presentation, based on the time allotted, the audience, and your presentation style.

❏ Title and word the text on your slides for easiest understanding and greatest impact.

❏ Use an agenda slide and a recap slide in every presentation, to make sure you "tell them what you're going to tell them" and "tell them what you told them."

❏ Vary the layout of your slides every three to five slides, with quotes, questions, charts, tables, symbols, clip art, photos, and/or video.

❏ Provide powerful handouts to serve as tangible takeaways that help your participants remember the content of your presentations and give the added value of extra information.

The Three Keys to Setting up a Great Slide Presentation

There are three keys to setting up a great presentation using PowerPoint or other software for the creation of slides to accompany what you say. I'm going to explain these keys in this chapter.

Key 1—Layout

Your layout is the first key factor to tackle when you begin to create your presentation. Consider your layout to be like the skeleton of your presentation. Just as our skeletons support our bodies, your layout should support your message and provide structure.

The easiest way to set up your layout is by using the PowerPoint masters, which are templates for your presentation. Using the masters is as easy as using your company letterhead. The letterhead is always set up for you: your logo, address, and other pertinent information are always there and they're always in the same place. This is the same principle for the masters.

There are two masters you need to set up in your presentation: the title master, which controls your title slides, and the slide master, which controls every other type of slide (i.e., bulleted list, chart, or blank slides).

Setting up Your Slide Master

On your PowerPoint standard toolbar, click View>Master>Slide Master. Your slide master will look almost identical to your slide. You will see all the sublevels of your bulleted text and you will see the text boxes for the date/time and footer and # for slide numbering. Again, this slide controls the layout of every slide in your presentation except the title slides. Because this master controls all the other slide layouts, it's important to maximize the use of white space on this master. All of your information—text, charts, and pictures—will be placed on the slides controlled by this master. If the master is too cluttered, you won't have enough space for all of your information.

> **White space** Any area on your slide that is not filled. The space doesn't have to be "white." For instance, your background may be a dark blue, but there are areas of your slide that are empty. That's considered to be "white space."

Here are some general guidelines to follow when you're setting up your slide master:

1. Select your title text box. Move it so the bottom of your title text box is no lower than 1.5" below the top of your slide. Go to View>Ruler to see your vertical and horizontal rulers.

2. Left-justify your title text in the text box. People read in a "Z" format. That is, they start at the top left and read to the right, then they make their way down to the bottom left and then across to the bottom right side of the slide, just like the shape of a "Z." It will help your audience start each slide in the correct place and make them feel at ease if your title text is left-justified in the text box. Go to Format>Alignment>Left.

3. Select your bulleted text box. Once it's selected, you'll see eight little white squares around the edge of the text box.

Place your cursor over the white square in the bottom right corner. (Your cursor will turn into a double-headed arrow.) Click and hold your mouse button down and drag the square down and to the right until it's about .25" from the right edge of the slide and from the footer text box. This will maximize the space you have for your bulleted text.

4. Move the top of your bulleted text box closer to the bottom of the title text box (almost touching). Make sure both the title and the bulleted text boxes are vertically aligned on the left. This will ensure that your bulleted text will be indented under your title.

5. Select the title text box. Place your mouse over the white square on the right in the center. Drag that side of the title text box to the right so it's even with the bulleted text box.

6. If you're going to be giving this presentation to individuals outside your company, then place a small version of your logo in the bottom right corner of the slide. This may mean that you have to move the #'s text box over to the left. The

Quick Ways to Select and Move Items

To select a text box, first make sure you have nothing else selected and you do not have a blinking cursor in the text box before you try to select it. To quickly select multiple items on your slide, hold down your shift key and then single-click any items to add them to your selection. If you need to select multiple small images, put your cursor above and to the left of the image in the top left corner. Then, while holding down the button, drag your mouse down and to the far right, creating an invisible rectangle around all of the pieces you want selected. When you have all of the pieces in the invisible rectangle, release the button and they will be selected.

If you want to deselect one of the multiple items you just selected, single-click the border of that item while still holding down your shift key. The easiest way to deselect all items is to click in the gray area surrounding your slide or an area of "white space."

To easily move selected items around, use your arrow keys. To move your items straight up or over, hold your shift key down, select the item while holding down your mouse button and the shift key, and move the item either up or down.

key to creating the perfect-size logo is to make the logo as small as you can and yet keep all the text readable.

Setting up Your Title Master

Here are three easy steps to create consistency on your title master:

1. Make sure your text is sans serif (see "Consistent Fonts" under Key 2) and the title and bullet fonts match those of the slide master.

2. Move your text boxes, if necessary, to fit the background.

3. Copy any elements you want to repeat on each slide from the slide master and then paste them onto the title master. This way, they will be in the same exact location on every slide.

> **Key Term**
>
> **Serif fonts** Fonts with small flourishes (called "serifs" extending from the main strokes of each letter, such as Times New Roman, Book Antiqua, Bookman Old Style, Calisto, and Garamond.
>
> **Sans serif fonts** Fonts that are straight and clean, without extraneous lines (no serifs), such as Arial, Century Gothic, Eras, Franklin Gothic, Helvetica, Lucida Sans, Tahoma, and Verdana.

Setting up Your Slides

Once you have your slide master and title master set up, it's time to set up your slides. To return to your slides, go to View>Slide.

When you lay out your slide properly, your audience will focus on the information and not its placement. One of the easiest ways to continue your layout from your masters to your slides is to create an invisible grid for your presentation. This helps you keep consistent in placing text, charts, and images. Break your presentation background into two or three equal columns with space in between. Use your guides in PowerPoint (View>Guides) to create your presentation grid.

First, start with a margin around your slide. For appearance and for printing, I try to stick to a .5" margin around my entire slide. To move your guides, simply place your cursor over the

Getting out of the Masters in PowerPoint 2000

When you're trying to return to your slides from your masters, go to View> Normal instead of View>Slide. This is sometimes confusing, but if you follow this step, it will be a lot easier for you to navigate within the presentation.

top of one of the guides, click and hold your mouse button, and drag the guide to create your margins. PowerPoint gives you two guides. To create more, hold your control key down and follow the same steps for moving the guides. This will duplicate that guide. Create either your two-column or three-column grid. Then, place at least three evenly spaced horizontal guides to break up the slide into sections. Now you have your grid for your entire presentation.

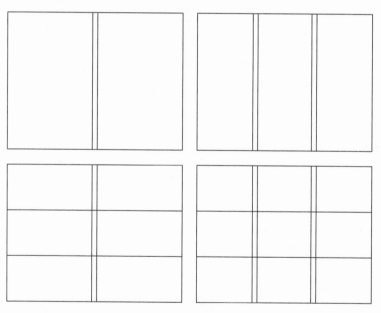

Figure 4-1. Slide layouts using PowerPoint

Key 2—Consistency

The second key to setting up your presentation is consistency. Consistency comes in many forms. You must be consistent in the following design elements:

- your placement of text and images,
- your font styles and sizes,
- your backgrounds,
- the style and treatment of your imagery,
- your charts.

Consistent Placement of Text and Images

Congratulations! Once you've set up your slide master and title master, you've won half the battle. Your masters keep the title, bulleted text, and charts in one place. Using your grid will also help you place subtitles, clip art, and other imagery consistently.

Consistent Fonts

You should use no more than three fonts per presentation: one for the title, one for the bulleted text, and another if you have special callout text on individual slides. Usually, I use only two fonts.

The two main classifications of fonts are *serif* and *sans serif* fonts. Serif fonts are best suited for printed materials, like brochures. Sans serif fonts are best suited for electronic presentations. How do you tell the difference between the two? Serif fonts have small flourishes extending from the main strokes of each letter. Sans serif fonts don't; they are straight and clean. This is why they are better for electronic presentations. Because there are extraneous lines, it's easier for the people at the back of the room to read your slides. Some examples of serif fonts are Times New Roman, Book Antiqua, Bookman Old Style, Calisto, and Garamond. Some examples of sans serif fonts are Arial, Century Gothic, Eras, Franklin Gothic, Helvetica, Lucida Sans, Tahoma, and Verdana.

Select the two sans serif fonts that will work best for your presentation. Do some tests. As you'll see, some fonts are wider than others, some are taller than others, and some have less space between letters than the other fonts. Try various combinations of fonts until you find the ones that best suit your presentation area and material.

For example, if your background takes space away from the left side of the slide, you have less space for your text. This usually affects your titles more than your bulleted text, so you may want to consider a condensed font like Arial Condensed for your title font.

Setting up Your Fonts

To set the fonts for the whole presentation, go to your slide master again: View>Master>Slide Master. If you followed the steps in "Key 1—Layout," your master layout should already be set. By properly placing your text boxes, your title text and bulleted text will be located in the same exact spot on each slide.

Your presentation default font is usually Times New Roman (the basic serif font), so we need to change it to a sans serif font. Select your title text box by holding down the shift key and single-clicking anywhere in the box, then click Format>Font. If you have your Formatting toolbar up, just click the drop-down font selector. Find and select the sans serif title font you've decided to use. Follow the same steps to change your bulleted text font.

Now that our fonts are correct, we need to address their

TRICKS OF THE TRADE

Quick Formatting Your Fonts

Here are two easy ways to globally change your fonts.

Every time you create a text box or symbol with text in it, you use your default font. Most presentations default to Times New Roman; we need to change that to a sans serif font, like Arial. The easiest way to change your default font is to go to your formatting toolbar and click the font drop-down. Locate and click Arial. That makes Arial your default font for this presentation. If you want to change the default size, just click the point-size drop-down (to the right of the fonts) and select a point size. Remember: before you can change your default, you cannot have anything else selected. Click in the gray area outside your slide to make sure of this.

To replace fonts in an existing presentation, go to Format>Replace Fonts. In the Replace Fonts window, click your top drop-down arrow. These are all of the fonts currently in the presentation. Select the font you want to change. Then, click the bottom box and find the new font. Click Replace to replace that font everywhere in that presentation with your new font. You can continue to do this until you've replaced all of the old fonts with new fonts.

size, known as *point size* or *font size*. The general rule is to keep your title font between 38 to 48 points. Fonts vary in width even if they're the same point size, since points measure font height.

> **Point** The unit used to measure font size (font height). There are 72 points in an inch. Most business letters are usually printed in 10, 11, or 12 points.

To decide what point size works best with your title, select a size that allows you to keep your titles on a single line. If you have to go under 38 points to fit your title on one line, either simplify your title text or change your title font on the slide master to a condensed sans serif font.

For your bulleted text, keep the point size between 24 and 32. When you're on the slide master, your presentation defaults to five levels of bulleted and sub-bulleted text. The first level of bulleted text is 32 points, the second level (this is the first sub-level bullet) is 28 points, and the third level (the second sub-level bullet) is 24 points.

> **How Big Is Big Enough?**
>
> What font sizes should you use for your slides? The consensus is that for normal text 18 points is the minimum, with recommendations generally being at least 22 or 24 points. For title text, experts tend to agree that at least 38 or 40 points is best. Size isn't all that matters, however: some fonts are easier to read than others, so you should use your judgment in following these guidelines.

It's best not to go beyond two sub-levels in your presentation. This means your bulleted text will consist of one main bullet with two sub-levels under it. The default point size of these bullets is fine; you shouldn't need to change their size.

The most important rule to remember with your bulleted text is the 8 x 8 rule explained in Chapter 3. Keep your bulleted text down to eight lines and try to make each line no more than eight words long. This will let you make optimal use of slide space while keeping your audience engaged. If you have too much text on your slides, your audience will become over-

Less Is Often More

Limit your bulleted lists, in number and in length. Bullets call attention to your words, but too many bullets and/or too many words will reduce that effect. Keep in mind the 8 x 8 rule: no more than eight lines and no line longer than eight words.

To Err Is Human

Smart Managing   Remember to check your spelling on every slide. Sure, it's easy to forget when you're caught up in the flow of putting together your presentation, with all the layout and design decisions. But it's not very hard. To use the spell check feature, pull down on the Tools menu and select "Spelling." Then, because you can't trust software to find all of your mistakes, read all text carefully to catch missing or repeated words or words used wrong.

whelmed and disinterested. Keep your bulleted text simple and to the point!

Ensuring accuracy takes time. But think of how embarrassing for you and distracting for your audience a misspelled word can be when it's up there in front of everybody at 38 points for several minutes.

Consistent Backgrounds

Every company should have a background set. The set should consist of four or five slides: cover, title, bullet, print, and chart. Your color scheme and animation should also be set on your masters.

The *cover slide* is the first slide members of your audience see when they walk into the presentation. This should have the least amount of text and the most graphics. (Figure 4-2 gives an example.)

The *title slide* should be used as the introduction slide for each new section. The title slide background should leave white space for a title and subtitle. The imagery can still be a little heavy or visible, as in Figure 4-3.

The *bullet slide* is used for most of the presentation. This slide's background should have the least amount of visible graphics, so you have no competition between the background and your text or pictures. (Figure 4-4).

Figure 4-2. An example of a cover slide.

Figure 4-3. An example of a title slide

Figure 4-4. An example of a bullet slide

The *chart slide* is, of course, used for charts. We'll get to them shortly.

If your background is dark or it is made up of images, you should also have a printer-friendly version of it, a *print slide.* This means you might take some of the images out of the background or change the dark color to white. You may leave some of the graphic or color detail on the bottom or left of the slide. You will then replace every slide, except the cover and title, with this print slide background before you print your presentation. This technique can be used for both color and black and white printed slides.

Consistent Style and Treatment of Imagery

Your images should complement your background and message. If you're giving a sales or marketing pitch, use photographs and actual pictures of your products or people. If it's a project/product update, you'll probably use a lot of symbols to represent items or processes. If the content is humorous, stick with clip art.

Once you decide which image type works best for your presentation, you must select a style for your images. For instance, if you use pictures, decide if they have a setting or they're alone. You may want to outline the images or put a drop shadow on them. For clip art, decide if your presentation calls for realistic clip art or cartoons. Some clip art has a heavy outline; some has no outline at all. If you use symbols, create them the same throughout the presentation. Use similar colors and style, such as hues of greens with a thick black outline.

Consistent Design of Charts

Create all of your charts alike. Once you set your slide color scheme (see "Setting Your Color Scheme," later in this chapter), your chart colors will be set for you. Your charts need to be either all 2-D or all 3-D. I generally recommend 2-D.

If you watch CNN, you know that all of the charts are 2-D. There's a reason for that. It's very important that the viewers quickly and easily understand the basic gist of the chart; they must be able to see the exact relationship between the numbers and their values. 3-D charts are skewed: their distorted perspective makes it hard to determine the exact value. If you need to show the exact value, use a 2-D chart. If the relationship between the items is more important than the exact value, use a 3-D chart. Figure 4-5 shows a bar chart done in 3-D and in 2-D.

Remember: keep the looks of all your charts consistent. Select either solid colors with outlines or gradients. Whatever you choose, make sure it contrasts well with the background.

Charts are a good way to break up your bulleted slides. Remember the recommendation from Chapter 3 to change your slide layout every three to five slides.

Charts: Q's and A's

Here are some common questions and answers about charts:

1. Should my charts be 2-D or 3-D?

Determine which perspective will present your data more simply and effectively and therefore be easier to read. Then be consistent.

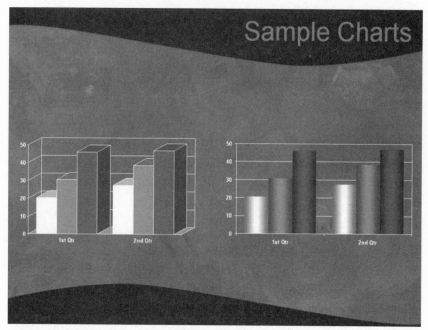

Figure 4-5. The same information in 3-D and 2-D versions

2. How can I decide which type of chart would best represent my data?

To show change over time, there are basically two choices. If you have more than four or five data points and/or you want to emphasize continuity over several months or years, it's probably best to use a *line chart*. If, however, you have fewer data points and you want to emphasize quantity at specific times, you should use a *column chart* (vertical bars). (Vertical bars work better than horizontal bars, because we naturally associate left-to-right orientation with the passing of time.)

If you want to show relationships among values, to compare several items at one point in time, use a *horizontal bar chart*.

For comparing parts of a whole (percentages or fractions) to show proportions, use a *pie chart*. Note, however, that a pie chart can be hard to read if there are more than five slices or if any of the slices are very thin. You can make a pie chart more dramatic by "exploding" one of the slices to highlight it.

3. I've got data for two years. Do I need to show all 24 months, rather than eight quarters?

Usually not in a chart. If anyone really needs the numbers, provide them in a separate printout, not a chart on a slide. Use just enough of the information to make your point: eight quarters should be enough—and 24 months would be overwhelming. Remember: you can always refer to your Notes Page for specific data and formulas.

4. How do I enhance the most important information in a chart?

You can enhance a piece of the pie or one of your lines by changing the color or filling that piece with a picture or texture, while keeping the rest of the chart all one color. The chart still shows the value relative to the others, but you're bringing out the one piece of information that's most important.

Key 3—Color

Color is the final key to setting up your presentation. Our colors set the mood, tone, reactions, and expectations for our presentations. Certain colors are best suited for your background, while others are better for foreground elements such as text or charts.

There are two families of colors, the "hot" and the "cool." The "hot" colors are reds, oranges, and yellows. These colors are best suited for your foreground elements. They draw attention. The "cool" colors are best suited for your background. These colors are blues, greens, and purples. They're also OK to use in foreground elements, but you have to make sure they're lighter or darker than the background color. If you want to use a "hot" color for your background, reduce the hotness by taking some of the saturation (intensity or purity) out of the color, so it's dull, not bright. Hot colors are not the best for backgrounds, but if you have to use them, this is the answer.

The Messages of Colors

Colors have subliminal messages. When you know what they represent, you'll know when and how to use them. The following are the emotional representations of the "hot" and "cool" family of colors plus white and black:

Blue. This is the most popular background color, because it's peaceful and soothing. It's linked with contemplation and patience. Blue is calm, credible, conservative, peaceful, and trusting. Since so many people like blue, it's a safe choice for a presentation. Blue is the background color of choice in over 90% of business presentations.

Green. This is an excellent background color for presentations that require interaction with the audience and/or feedback. It's restful and refreshing. Green is harmonious, envious, growth, money, and relaxation. Also use it as a highlight color.

Purple. Another good background color, purple is impressive and spiritual and encourages vitality. Use darker shades for backgrounds and lighter shades for accents. But be careful: too much of the lighter shades of purple can be detracting because it tends to be humorous. Purple is vital, spiritual, whimsy, humorous, and detracting.

Red. Red is hot! It's a dominant color that calls attention to the message and stimulates audiences to take action. Red is motivating, but also represents pain. As an accent color, it works well to catch and hold attention. A note on financial presentations: don't use red as an accent color for bullets or numbers—you'll definitely send the wrong message, since red in accounting traditionally means loss, not profit.

Orange. Another hot color, orange is an excellent contrast color against a dark background and a good choice for text or accents. It's a powerful and cheerful color that encourages communication. Orange is happy, concentrating, intelligent, and rebellious. Use orange as an accent color.

Yellow. The last hot color, yellow stimulates the brain and promotes decisiveness. Use yellow for text or accents—it's an excellent contrast color against a dark background. Yellow is bright, cheerful, enthusiastic, optimistic, and warm. Use yellow in text and bullets, but be careful: big areas of bright yellow can be irritating.

White. White is usually used as a text color with dark blue and other dark backgrounds. You can use it for titles or text. White represents a fresh canvas, but add some accent colors if you use it as the main background color. White is freshness, new, innocent, neutral, and pure.

Black. Black symbolizes a clean slate. It's used for emphasis and is associated with finality. Black is sophisticated, independent, emphatic, and final. Large areas of black add emphasis and highlight your information. It can be used as the center frame for a background.

Setting Your Color Scheme

By now, you should have an idea of the colors you want to use for your presentation. The presentation should have about three main colors and four accent colors. Your three main colors should be used for your background, title, and bullet text and main images. For instance, you may choose dark blue for your background, gold for your title text, bullets, and image outlines,

---

Concern for the Color-Challenged

Red means stop and greens means go, right? Not for all people.

About 10% of males and less than 1% of females have a color perception defect known as color blindness. This is an inaccurate term for a lack of perceptual sensitivity to certain colors. There are three types of color receptors in our eyes: red, green, and blue. We also have black and white receptors. Color blindness results from a lack of one or more of the types of color receptors. Most color perception defects are for red or green or both. Another form of color blindness— yellow-blue—is extremely rare.

People who are color-challenged depend of the intensity of colors, on dark and light. They may see them as shades of gray, but they can distinguish. The most common color perception problems are with certain combinations, such as yellow on green, green on red, red on green, blue on red, red on blue, and red on black.

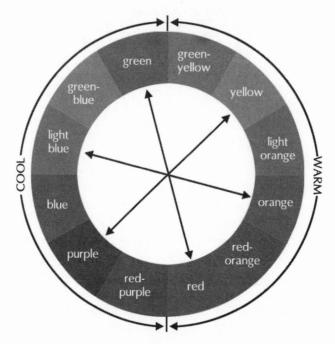

Figure 4-6. Color wheel showing complementary colors

and white for your bulleted text. The other colors you choose should be used in charts, graphics, clip art, and any other imagery. Try to select colors that are complementary to one another. Notice on the color wheel (Figure 4-6) that blue and yellow are complementary; that's why they work well together. Use complementary colors for your four accent colors. When you use the "cool" colors, make sure you select a lighter shade, because it needs to pop out from the dark blue background.

> **Key Term** **Complementary** Specifically, characteristic of two colors that are directly opposite each other on the color wheel, such as blue and orange, red and green, or yellow and violet. Generally, a term used to characterize two or more colors that work well together.

PowerPoint makes it easy for us to use the colors we've selected. It allows us to change our presentation color scheme so we can use the colors over and over again.

Here's how. Go to Format>Slide Color

Scheme. The Color Scheme pop-up window appears. It has two tabs, Standard and Custom. The first tab shows the standard color schemes for this template. Click the Custom tab and you'll see all of the colors available and how each one affects your presentation. The colored boxes represent that item. The top box color is the color of your background. The second box is the color of your bulleted text and any lines. The third box is your shadow color. The fourth box down is the color of your title text. The fifth box is the color of all your AutoShapes and it's the first color of your charts. The last three colors are more colors for your charts and they affect your hyperlinks.

You can select any one of the colored squares and click Change Color. This brings up another pop-up window with a Standard and Custom tab. You can select a standard color or click the Custom tab and make your own color. Once you've changed the default colors to your new color scheme, you can make this scheme your default. Click the button Add as Standard Scheme and it will become an option on the Standard tab in this window. This is where you would incorporate your company colors.

If you have certain PMS colors that you need to incorporate into your presentation, here's how. First, you will need the RGB (red, green, blue) conversion from the PMS colors. Someone in your marketing or graphics department should be able to give you this information. On your Custom tab in Color Scheme (Figure 4-7), select the color you want to change; click Change Color and then the Custom tab. In the bottom right of the window, you'll see Red, Green, and Blue. Type your numbers into these boxes and then click OK. It's just as easy as that!

Contrast of Colors

Contrast also plays a big role in your presentation. If people cannot see the dif-

> **PMS colors** Colors numbered in a universally accepted recognition system called Pantone Matching System, created by Pantone Inc., the company that pioneered color standards for the textiles and apparel industries.

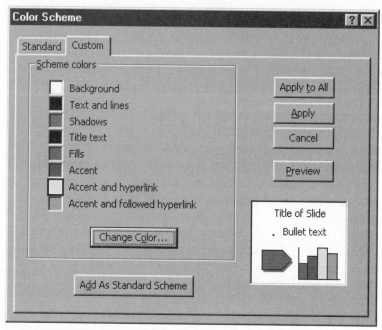

Figure 4-7. Color scheme dialog box

ference between the color of the text and the color of the back-ground, how are they going to understand or focus on your message? You have to make sure there's optimal contrast between text and background. For electronic presentations, light text on a dark background is best. A dark blue background with yellow text is the most popular combination, used in over 90% of all business presentations.

Of course, if any members of your audience have defective color perception, contrast may be the only way they can under-stand your presentation.

Get a Little Help

So, there you have it: the three keys to setting up a great pres-entation—layout, consistency, and color. You're now ready to move on to Chapter 5, "The Basics of Designing High-Impact Presentations."

If you're unsure about what you're doing, you should remember that you don't have to design your presentations alone. Sure, you can ask colleagues, friends, and family members for their opinions. But you can also get help from PowerPoint, through automatic style checking.

In PowerPoint 97, you can check a presentation for consistency and style by selecting Tools/Style Checker. PowerPoint 2000, by default, automatically checks your presentation for consistency, style, and visual clarity and marks problems on a slide with a light bulb.

To use the light bulb, you've got to have the Office Assistant on. To turn on the Assistant, select Help/Show the Office Assistant.

To use style checking, open your presentation, click the light bulb, and then click the option you want in the list. You can change the options included in the style checking. First, select Change style checker options for all presentations. Then, select, clear, or change the options you want on the Case and End Punctuation and Visual Clarity tabs. If you decide to reset the default settings, just click Defaults on each tab.

Style checking can help you avoid some of the common mistakes in your slides, so your presentation will look more professional display for little effort. If the light bulb appears when you switch to a slide, click on it for some advice on that slide. The light bulb will appear if you're using too many fonts, if the text is too small, if a slide contains too many bullet points, or if your use of capitalization and punctuation is inconsistent. (You can change any of the settings for this feature, through Tools>Options>Spelling and Style>Style Options.)

Manager's Checklist for Chapter 4

❏ The first step in setting up your layout is to create your title master and your slide master. Then continue your layout from your masters to your slides by creating an invisible grid to guide you as you place text, charts, and images.

❑ Be consistent with your design elements: your placement of text and images, your font styles and sizes, your backgrounds, the style and treatment of your imagery, and your charts.

❑ Make it easier for your participants to get the most out of your presentation by choosing font sizes and styles with care and by following the 8 x 8 rule with your bullet text.

❑ Consistency with graphics—background, charts, tables, images—is crucial. Differences that have no intentional significance tend to distract and participants may consciously or unconsciously infer significance.

❑ When you choose your colors, keep in mind that the colors in a presentation set the mood, tone, reactions, and expectations. Remember, too, that not all people are able to distinguish all colors—which makes the use of contrasting darks lights all the more important.

The Basics of Designing High-Impact Slide Presentations

A s you progress through this book, your presentation should become stronger and more solidified. By now, you should have great text in a great format using proper fonts. You should know the guidelines for selecting colors and you should know what type of images and charts to use to keep the presentation consistent.

Is there more to design? Of course. Now we need to ask ourselves, "Why am I designing this presentation?" That question breaks down into three questions:

- Am I designing it for my audience?
- Am I designing it for my image?
- Am I designing it for the objective of the presentation?

By asking yourself these three questions, you determine the next step toward designing a high-impact presentation. This means that you're designing your presentation in terms of your audience, your image, or the objective of the presentation.

Design for Your Audience, Your Image, and Your Objective

This is the basic principle of designing a presentation: design for your audience, image, and objective. These three purposes should affect every aspect of your presentation—the medium you chose to use to deliver the message, the colors you choose, your style of design and imagery, the amount of text on your slides, the way you organize your information, etc.

Designing for Your Audience

What does it mean to design for your audience? Here's an example.

Let's say you're giving a presentation to the VP of marketing and her staff to persuade them to add a new promotion to help the summertime sales of a new product in your region. This is a promotion that will work only in your region of the company.

First, you're dealing with the whole marketing team, so they know the tricks for creating persuasion, which means you have to use the tricks on them.

Start with your colors. What color would you use for your background? Would you use purple? (Refer to the section in Chapter 4, "The Messages of Colors.") Would you use blue? Or maybe you should even try using the company colors. This will really impress them. Let's say the company colors are navy and gold. Great! So, you would use navy for the background and gold for the title text and accents.

How about the style of the presentation for this audience? Should it have a light whimsical flair or should it be serious? You need to be the judge of this. If you get along well with the marketers, you may want to add a bit of humor or lightheartedness to this slightly delicate subject. But, if you're known for always asking for more, keep it simple, straightforward, and to the point.

These considerations also affect the design of the presentation. Is clip art appropriate? Does your company have stock imagery you can use? Or does this call for you being a little more resourceful? Here are two ideas:

Where to Find Additional Media Resources

There are several Web sites where you can purchase stock imagery. A good resource for imagery and more is BizPresenter.com. The company sells PowerPoint templates, stock photography, *New Yorker* cartoons (if you can add that flair of humor, maybe to your opening), and professional illustrations. It evens offer the service of taking the presentation from you and creating a custom-designed presentation. The Web site—www.bizpresenter.com—has a power browse feature, so you just type in what you want (e.g., "money") and up pop great images.

- Buy or borrow a digital camera and take pictures of the location, the product, or whatever else will help the marketers see your vision.
- Purchase stock imagery.

When it comes to your content, keeping your audience in mind can mean the life or death of your presentation. For our marketers, we want two levels of information.

The main presentation consists of top-level details only, i.e., What's the benefit for marketing? Will this move into other marketing efforts in your area? How will this affect your current marketing budget? Are

Read Before You Buy

Be careful when purchasing stock imagery. Read the licensing agreement before you buy. Some of the companies will let you use their imagery only in certain instances. Here's an example: "You may not use XXX material to directly advertise or directly promote any product or service or use XXX material in any presentation, service, or product that is offered for sale." Ouch! It pays to read the fine print.

you asking to reallocate or are you asking for new funding? What will marketing have to do to support you? How much of their resources will they need to allocate—personnel, collateral, production costs, etc.?

Then, be prepared for the additional questions with extra slides, which you keep hidden, to pull out as needed. These slides are for details that the others might be interested in.

You want to make sure that you stick to the 8 x 8 rule, which you remember from Chapter 4: no more than eight lines of bullets and no more than eight words per line. (This may vary a little, depending on the font you've selected for the presentations. Narrow fonts will allow you to get more words per line, sometimes even up to 12 words per line.) The point is to keep it brief and concise.

Again, make sure to keep sentence structure parallel. Start each bullet with either a noun or a verb and keep them in the same tense (either past or present) and voice (active or passive). Some of this information is probably better represented graphically, so add charts and pictures and minimal text.

What about time? Do you normally have a lot of time in front of a VP? Usually not. You're lucky if you have 20 minutes in which to educate and persuade your audience to see your view and get buy-in from them.

Here are some things to remember when presenting to top management:

1. Even if you have 30 minutes allotted, try to keep it to 10-15 minutes and make your point in the first three minutes. This will give you plenty of time for Q&A and they will be even happier if they break earlier than expected.
2. Keep the information on the top level. Do not display drill-down detailed information—but have it available in case someone asks.

Designing for Your Image

Sometimes it's important to reflect in your presentations the type of company or department you represent. Let's take an example.

You're the main account rep for a marketing firm. You and your team are doing a pitch for one of your best customers, to sell them on this new marketing/design strategy you've created for them. Companies that hire marketing firms expect a lot from them. They expect creativity and innovation. They look at everything you do, because if *your* image doesn't appeal to them, then how can you make *their* image appealing?

Figure 5-1 shows an example of a slide you've created to tell them the main points of this new strategy. It looks more like an overhead than a slide projected through a LCD projector. How can we fix this slide to better display our image?

Marketing Communications Strategies

Enhance current external marketing plan to maximize consumer awareness

Develop promotions and events to increase frequency of visits and/or average expenditure

Merchandise Grand Opening throughout the center - both internally and externally

Reinforce new positioning throughout all communication

Develop a proactive public relations campaign to complement p.r. efforts

Establish measurement tools to gauge program effectiveness

Figure 5-1. Example of poorly designed slide listing strategies

Remember, they're looking to you as the experts in creating identity and a unique image. This slide's design doesn't reflect that about your company. Compare it with the slide in Figure 5-2. Much different!

The first thing you can do is create a new background. Your company colors are blue and green, so you've created a background using both colors. The background is innovative and different. It now tells more about who you are ... a top-notch marketing company with people who think out of the box.

What about the text on the original slide? This is supposed to be the overview slide. You're supposed to be telling them briefly what you'll do for them. This is too much information. Notice how the text in the second slide is condensed. There are now only four bullet points instead of six. Each bullet point is only three or four words long. Plus, you've used parallel sentence structure. Each bullet point starts with a verb in the present

Figure 5-2. Redesigned slide to emphasize new strategies

tense. The presentation is now to the point about the marketing strategy for this customer.

To add to the design, semi-transparent rectangles have been added in PowerPoint under each bullet point to help distinguish each of them as important steps. Finally, to enhance the design even further, a drop-cap "M" has been added to the title.

The slide now better represents who you are. It's clean, crisp, to the point, innovative, and well designed. The color selections make you look wise (blue) and yet make your audience want to participate (green).

Designing for Your Objective

What is the objective of your presentation? Is it to persuade, to train, to entertain?

Let's say you're director of HR and you're creating a recruiting presentation. The objective of this presentation is to persuade your invited guests to come work for you. You're trying to tell this audience that you're different from everyone else. You have this meeting once a year all over the country, trying to hire the best of the best. Normally, you give little or no thought to designing the presentation. It's just text on slides, something for you to talk from.

Figure 5-3 is a slide from your normal presentation. It's the slide that lets the guests know about how your company would compensate them.

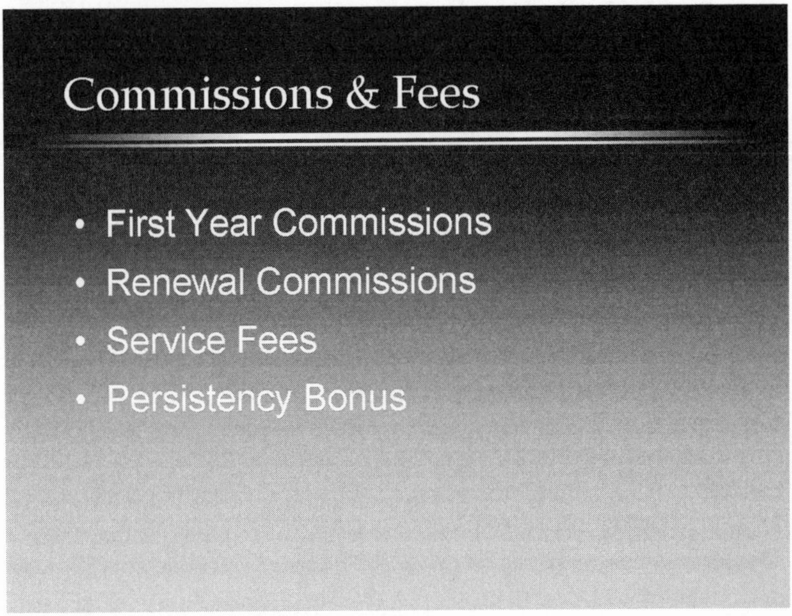

Figure 5-3. Example of slide on topic of compensation

Let's pull it apart and see if our design helps our objective. Remember: we're trying to let the audience know that we're different from every other company that wants to hire them.

Unfortunately, our background selection says otherwise. We've chosen a basic PowerPoint template. It's one they've all seen a hundred times. They've probably even given their own presentations using this background. This shows we are not very original and it defeats the purpose of our objective. Not only did we use a basic PowerPoint template, but we also selected the template with a purple color scheme. Is purple the best color for our objective? (Refer to Chapter 4, under "Key 3—Color.") Purple can be humorous or even detract from our message. So, the color of the background isn't helping us achieve our objective. Subliminally, our guests are not taking this presentation very seriously because of our color selection.

Here's a very easy way to change this slide so that it helps us meet our objective. In Figure 5-4, we started with the background. This is not a PowerPoint template; we created this background using a green and black gradient (Format> Background>Fill Effects>Gradient). Why did we choose green? If you recall, green means harmony, growth, and relaxation. These emotions help us to meet our objective. This color will put our guests at ease so they're more likely to participate in the presentation. Green also means growth, so they'll feel a sense of growing with this company.

The objective of this individual slide is to make the guests aware of our unique compensation package. This slide deserves

Figure 5-4. Redesigned slide on topic of compensation

Questions of Perspective

If you've been doing a presentation for a while or even just preparing a presentation, you lose perspective. It's a good idea to test it out.

Ask some people outside the project—even friends and family members—to serve as a focus group. Briefly explain the objective(s) of the presentation and your target, then give the presentation. Afterwards, ask for comments.

This can be difficult, so be open and encourage any reactions. Don't give explanations or react in any way to their input; when someone contributes, thank him or her and take notes. After all comments have been shared, thank your focus group for helping you.

---

some special treatment to help emphasize this point. We kept it simple by adding a black box in the center, emphasizing the information in the box. We also show how important each one of the four items is by separating them out into their own boxes. Finally, we added the company logo to really make the audience understand who is offering such a unique and wonderful compensation package.

Using Your Corporate Identity

Whether you're designing for your audience, for your image, for the objective of the presentation, or (ideally) for all three purposes, you want to use your corporate identity—logo, typography, colors, and graphic style—to its greatest advantage.

Most companies spend quite a bit of their budget on marketing. They hire companies to create a "look" specific to them. This look tells who they are and what they are about. It should distinguish them from anyone else. They go to the expense of designing and printing materials to give to clients, to educate employees, etc. Companies have also realized the need to incorporate this identity into their Web sites. So, they're starting to see the need to incorporate their identity into electronic media.

But one of the biggest electronic media tools out there is a PowerPoint presentation. More than 90% of presenters use PowerPoint. Unfortunately, most companies are still allowing

The Power of Corporate Identity

Think of Apple Computers and you imagine the apple logo. Think of Volkswagen and the "VW" symbol comes to mind immediately. Nike and its "swoosh" logo, Michelin and the Man, Mercedes-Benz and its three-point emblem, IBM and its block letters .... The list goes on of companies that have a strong corporate identity, a look. Any representative from any of these companies would definitely use that look in any presentation.

Maybe your organization is not as well-known as these examples. But none of them started out famous—and an important part of their success is marketing their identity.

their presenters to use the templates that come with Microsoft PowerPoint. The result: they're displaying PowerPoint's identity, not their own.

Take advantage of your resources! If your company has spent the money to create a corporate identity, then use it! You have some alternatives. First, you can ask your marketing department to create a PowerPoint template for you that's consistent with the corporate identity. If you know this won't happen or you don't have an in-house marketing department, then you'll have to take matters into your own hands. You have two choices here:

- Purchase a background.
- Create your own background.

Purchasing Backgrounds

There are a handful of companies like ours, Creative Minds, Inc., that create custom backgrounds for those who do not have the resources. Some of these companies create custom backgrounds, some create generic topic-specific backgrounds, and others do a combination of both. Your future needs and budget will dictate which you use. If you have the budget, we recommend having a background created specifically for you.

Here are some things you need to be aware of when purchasing backgrounds:

- If you won't be altering the background image, it's best to purchase a PowerPoint template file (filename.pot), rather than an image file.
- If you purchase image files for your backgrounds, make sure they are in a JPEG (filename.jpg) format and they are designed in a low resolution (72 dpi).

JPEG A standardized image compression mechanism for compressing color or gray-scale digital images of real-world scenes. JPEG (pronounced "jay-peg") stands for Joint Photographic Experts Group, the committee that wrote the standard. JPEG does not work very well on non-realistic images, such as cartoons or line drawings.

dpi Dots per inch, a measure of resolution for images and printing.

Creating Backgrounds

If you have the resources yourself to create a background, then go for it! You need to have a photo-editing software package, corporate collateral, corporate images, corporate colors, and your corporate logo with a logo standards kit (if there are standards for use). Once you have these, you're ready to go.

Here are a few things you need to know when creating the image for your background:

Going Outside

Smart Managing

Sometimes you have to go outside your company to specialists in order to get what you need. You can find generic backgrounds that aren't very expensive. So, if budget is an issue, this may be the alternative. Be careful: these backgrounds are available to everyone, so you may get back into the "déjà vu" syndrome that people have when they use PowerPoint backgrounds.

If you can get a budget, have a template created specifically for your company or department. If you don't have the budget, approach others in the company to see if you can combine budgets to purchase this resource. Most marketing departments will love the fact that you are creating consistency by incorporating your corporate identity into your presentations. They may even chip in too.

- Keep the resolution at 72 dpi. This will give you the resolution you need for an electronic presentation while keeping the file size down.
- Keep the canvas size to the size of your computer screen resolution. If your computer is set to 800 x 600, then make your canvas size in the software package you're using to create the background 800 x 600.
- Color depths usually aren't an issue any more, but make sure the mode of color you use is RGB (red, green, and blue). This is compatible with your projector.

Once you've created your background, you can turn it into a PowerPoint template. Here are things you need to know when creating a POT:

- Make sure that you use the slide master and title master to format your entire presentation (View>Masters>...).
- When adding your backgrounds to the masters, do not Insert>Picture. Go to Format>Background and click the down arrow in this pop-up box. Then, select Fill Effects, the Picture tab in the new window, and the Select Picture button. Locate the background you've created, then click OK twice and Apply once. If you click Apply to all, that will apply this background to the title master as well.
- Set up your Slide Color Scheme. (See Chapter 4, under "Key 3—Color.")

Resources at Your Fingertips

Most of you probably already have the tool you need to create your own background. It's a photo-editing software package by Microsoft that comes *free* with the Office Suite, Microsoft Photo Editor. If you don't have it on your computer, get the CD or ask your system administrator to load it for you. It should be located in the Value Pack folder of the CD. You can do many things with Photo Editor. You can create your own backgrounds by importing pictures and using some of the filters and you can alter imagery for using within your presentation body.

- Set the animations on your text in your masters (Slide Show>Custom Animation). Keep the animations simple, such as the Wipes Left.
- If you're going to distribute this template file to others, you want to create a

> **Key Term**
>
> **POT** A PowerPoint template that defines the style of your entire presentation. It's the background, the colors, and even the animation. To apply your PowerPoint template to a new or existing presentation, go to Format>Apply Design. In the pop-up window you can locate your POT files. Select the template you've created and click Apply to apply these attributes to your entire presentation.

PowerPoint template (filename.pot). You do this by selecting File>Save As. In the pop-up window, click the down arrow next to Type and locate Presentation Template. This will save the file as filename.pot instead of filename.ppt.

Now that you know the basics of presentation design, let's move into adding pizzazz!

Guidelines

You should now have all the guidelines and resources necessary to move into the last phase of your presentation design. That's adding the pizzazz. But, before you move on, here's a

> ### Adobe Photoshop Elements
>
> **Tricks of the Trade**
>
> If you don't have a photo-editing software package, don't fret. Adobe Photoshop Elements is the new kid on the block among photo-editing software packages for the presentation designer. Elements offers simple-to-use features yet keeps its punch just like its big brother Photoshop 6. The interface is similar to Photoshop 6, but Elements has user-friendly features such as the recipes palette, which shows how to do it and can also do it for you. It helps you prepare images for print, e-mail, or posting on the Web. Elements is very inexpensive, a fraction of the price of its big brother Photoshop 6. Visit www.adobe.com/products/photoshopel/main.html for more information.

quick checklist to make sure you followed the guidelines in this chapter:

- Are you designing for your audience, your image, or your objective?
- Did you determine if your company already has a corporate template?
- If there's no corporate template, did you use the corporate identity to create one or have one made?
- Did you use the rules for designing your own background?
- Did you save your PowerPoint template in the correct format?

Manager's Checklist for Chapter 5

❑ If you want to design a high-impact presentation, you've got to start with the question, "Why am I designing this presentation? For my audience? For my image? For the objective of the presentation?" The answer should affect every aspect of your presentation.

❑ If you're designing for your audience, think about their experience, their expectations, the content they want and need, and the style most likely to work.

❑ If you're designing for your image, think about what participants expect of you and how you can meet the positive expectations and counter the negative expectations.

❑ If you're designing for your objective, think of every aspect of your content and design in terms of that objective, whether it's to persuade, to train, to entertain, and so on.

❑ Whether you're designing for your audience, for your image, for the objective of the presentation, or (ideally) for all three purposes, you want to use your corporate identity to its greatest advantage in your presentation.

Adding Pizzazz to Your Slide Presentation

By now, you should have your content organized, your template designed, and your information in the presentation. Now it's time to add pizzazz!

Pizzazz is what helps us grab attention and helps the members of our audience retain the information in our presentation. Pizzazz comes in many forms and styles. You can add symbols, clip art, images, charts, sound, and even video.

There are two things to keep in mind when you're choosing the type of pizzazz you want to add:

- Will this help my audience better understand my message?
- Will this match my presentation style?

Symbols

The most basic piece of pizzazz you can add to your presentation is a symbol. You can use a symbol to represent an idea, a product, a service, etc.

For example, instead of creating a bulleted slide that com-
pares Corporation ABC and Corporation XYZ, use symbols to
represent them, as in Figure 6-1.

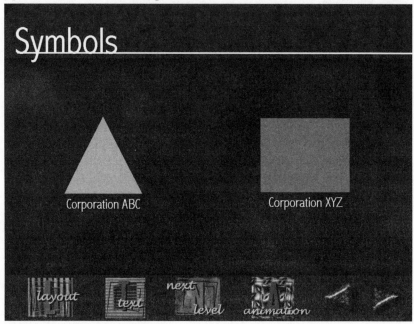

Figure 6-1. Using symbols

Symbols off the Shelf

PowerPoint has many basic symbols already available to use.
On the Drawing Toolbar, usually on the bottom of your screen in
PowerPoint, there's an AutoShapes pop-up menu. Here you'll
find the tools you need to draw or add symbols. After you draw
one of the symbols, you may notice a yellow triangle appears.
This triangle will allow you to change your image in some way.
Normally, you can only scale or distort your symbol, but this triangle will let you skew or otherwise change the perspective of
the symbol.

For instance, let's say you select the octagon under Basic
Shapes. After you draw your octagon, you can drag the yellow
triangle to the left to lengthen the horizontal and vertical sides
and make the octagon more like a box or drag it to the right to

lengthen the diagonal sides and make the octagon more like a diamond (Figure 6-2).

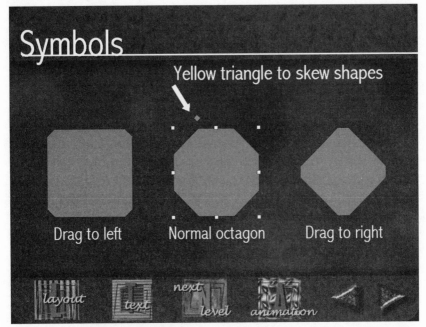

Figure 6-2. Making symbols

Filling a Symbol

Once you've created the appropriate symbol, you can fill it. In PowerPoint, you have five options for fills:

- solid color
- gradient
- texture
- pattern
- picture

Solid color. Here's how to fill your symbol with a solid color. First, select the symbol by single-clicking it. Then, on the Drawing Toolbar at the bottom of your PowerPoint screen, click the down-arrow to the right of the paint can and a color menu will pop up. The eight colors that appear are the colors that are defined in your slide Color Scheme. (See Chapter 4 for details on how to change colors.) The AutoShape should already be filled with the fifth color from the left. (This is the fill color from the Color Scheme.) To change the color of your new shape, select More Fill Colors. Your Colors window will pop up, with two tabs, Standard or Custom. You can select a standard color or click the Custom tab and make a color to fill your symbol.

You can also fill your symbol with a color that is semitransparent. First, select the color for your symbol. Then, in the bottom left corner of the Color pop-up window, check the box next to Semitransparent.

To fill your symbol with any of the other options (gradient, texture, pattern, or picture), click on the down-arrow to the right of the paint can. In the pop-up menu, select Fill Effects. This will bring up the Fill Effects window (Figure 6-3). In the window, you'll see four tabs: Gradient, Texture, Pattern, and Picture.

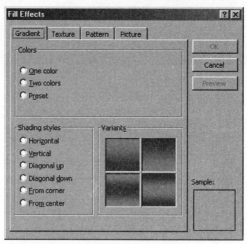

Figure 6-3. The full effects window in PowerPoint

Gradient. On the Gradient tab, you have three choices. You can select one color and then mix it with percentages of white or black. You can select two colors from the PowerPoint Color window and mix them or make your own colors. You can also select Preset and you have 16 preset gradients. Be careful if you use the preset: the gradients don't provide good contrast if you have text over your symbol. While you're creating your gradient, you can click the Preview button to see how the gradient will look in your symbol.

Texture. Under the Texture tab, there are 24 options. When using the textures, make sure that they work with your presentation design. For instance, if yours is a financial company and your template includes some strong imagery, such as a big building or Wall Street, use the green marble texture as a fill for some of your symbols to keep it consistent.

Pattern. When filling a symbol with a pattern, try to keep the pattern simple enough so it doesn't distract your audience. Also, symbols filled with the thin horizontal or vertical lines can sometimes appear as "noise" through some projectors: your image will seem to vibrate on the screen.

Picture. If you fill a symbol with a picture, make sure that the picture is in low resolution (72 dpi). You usually want to use JPEGs (.jpg). TIFFs (.tif) are also a popular file format, but the file size can be as much as three times larger than a JPEG.

When you're filling a symbol with a picture, the picture will be scaled to fit into that shape. For instance, if the symbol is shorter than the picture you're placing inside, the picture will appear to be squished.

> **TIFF** Tagged Image File Format, a non-proprietary tag-based image file format that's an industry standard for data communication implemented by most scanner manufacturers and desktop publishing applications. The TIFF format originated in 1986 when Aldus Corporation (makers of PageMaker) and leading scanner vendors worked together to create a standard file format for images used in desktop publishing.

Creating a Symbol

If none of the symbols that PowerPoint offers work for you, you can draw your own. On the Draw Toolbar under AutoShapes, go to Lines (Figure 6-4) and use the bottom three options: Curve, Freeform, or Scribble.

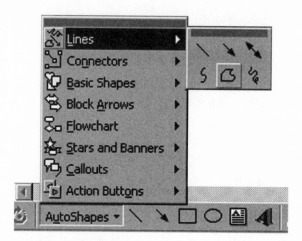

Figure 6-4. The draw toolbar

If you click Curve, your cursor will turn into a cross hair. Just start clicking and you'll create your symbol. This symbol will have curved edges at every click-point.

If you click Freeform and click the cross-hair cursor on the slide, you can both click and click-drag to create a symbol. The symbol will have hard edges.

With Scribble, you hold down your mouse button and draw, just like drawing with a pen. When you stop holding down the button, your drawing ends. Even if you don't come back to where you began, you can still fill your symbol. You can fill any of these symbols you've drawn the same way as filling PowerPoint's AutoShapes.

You can also add a drop shadow or add 3-D depth to your symbols (although you can't do both at the same time), by choosing 3-D Settings or Shadow Settings at the far right of the AutoShapes toolbar (Figure 6-5).

Figure 6-5. AutoShapes toolbar

Here's how to add a drop shadow:

- Single-click your symbol.
- On the Draw Toolbar, select the second icon from the right, for the Shadow Settings pop-up menu.
- Select any one of the 20 preset drop shadows or click the Shadow Settings button.
- If you choose Shadow Settings, a toolbar will appear. The first icon on the toolbar turns the shadow on and off. The next four allow you to move the shadow around the symbol. The last icon allows you to change the shadow color or make the color semitransparent.

This is how to add 3-D:

- Single-click your symbol.
- On the Draw Toolbar, select the last icon on the right, for the 3-D Settings pop-up menu.
- Select any one of the 20 preset 3-D settings or click the 3-D Settings button.
- If you choose 3-D Settings, a toolbar will appear. The first icon on the toolbar turns the 3-D on and off. The next four allow you to change the direction of the symbol. The sixth icon changes the depth of the 3-D. The seventh icon changes the direction. The eighth icon changes the lighting. The ninth changes the surface material. And the last icon allows you to change the 3-D color.

Text as a Symbol

The last type of symbol you can use in PowerPoint is WordArt. WordArt is text that you can fill and manipulate like a symbol.

To insert WordArt, go to the Draw Toolbar and click the tilted 3-D "A" (just to the left of the paint bucket). This will bring up the WordArt Gallery pop-up window. (See Figure 6-6.)

From here, you may select one of the predefined formats or just select the plain format in the top left corner and click the OK button. This will bring up the Edit WordArt Text pop-up window. Type your text, change your typeface and point size, and click the OK button.

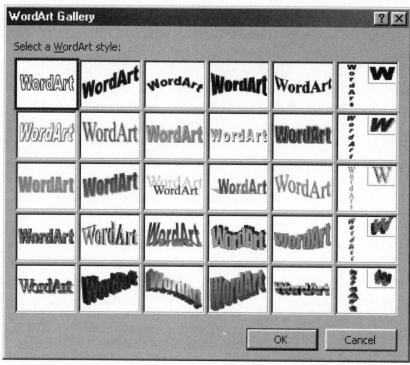

Figure 6-6. WordArt gallery

Once you've inserted WordArt into the presentation, you may manipulate it just like a symbol. You can use the yellow diamond to skew it. You can fill it with any color, gradient, texture, pattern, or picture. You can make it bigger or smaller, add a drop shadow, or make it 3-D.

WordArt also has its own toolbar, so you can make changes. Click the WordArt and the toolbar will appear. (If it doesn't, then go to View>Toolbars>WordArt.) The first icon on the toolbar lets you insert a piece of WordArt. The second icon lets you go back and edit your text. The third icon opens up the WordArt Gallery. The fourth icon formats the WordArt with fill and line colors. The fifth icon lets you change the shape of the WordArt. For instance, if you want text to wrap around the top of a circle, you would change the shape of the WordArt to an Arch Up curve. The sixth icon lets you rotate WordArt. The seventh icon changes the letter height. The eighth icon changes the WordArt to vertical text. The ninth icon changes the alignment. The tenth icon changes the spacing of the letters.

Clip Art

Clip art or illustrations are the next step up from symbols. Clip art better represents your message, but it's still abstract. Clip art comes in a variety of styles, from silly cartoons to professional illustrations. Clip art, in the form of a professional illus-
tration, is good to use to represent a concept or product that isn't created. The cartoons have their place, too. They can be used to lighten up a meeting or as an icebreaker in the opening of the presentation.

> *Key Term*
>
> **Clip art** Any ready-made graphic designed for use in presentations, publications, or Web pages. Clip art (also *clip-art* or *clipart*) includes illustrations, photos, and visual elements such as bullets, lines, and text separators. Also called *clip media.*

Finding Clip Art

PowerPoint comes with a library of clip art. Just choose Insert>Picture>ClipArt or click the Insert Clip Art button. In the Clip Art Gallery, scroll down the list of topics on the left and select a topic. In the clip art preview window, double-click click your choice to insert it on the open slide. Then close the Clip Gallery.

There are many other resources for good clip art. The first place you can look is on the Microsoft Web site. To get there from PowerPoint, go to Insert>Picture>ClipArt. This will bring up the Microsoft Clip Gallery window. In PowerPoint97, click the globe and magnifying glass icon in the bottom right corner, then follow the prompts to the Microsoft site. In PowerPoint2000, click the Clips Online button and follow the prompts to the site.

Here are some other Web sites you can visit to buy clip art and illustrations:

- www.bizpresenter.com
- www.eyewire.com
- www.arttoday.com

> **CAUTION!**
>
> **Read the Fine Print**
> Be sure to read the license agreement to make sure that you can use the imagery to suit your needs. As we mentioned in Chapter 5, the fine print can be restrictive. For example: "This is a perpetual license at will and can be terminated by ABC Clip Art at any time. ...This license will terminate automatically without notice from ABC Clip Art if you fail to comply with any provision of this license. Upon termination, you shall destroy all content or copies thereof." So, know what you're getting and how you can use it!

There are plenty of Web sites that offer free clip art—but you get what you pay for!

Formats

Most clip art is created as a WMF (windows metafile). This is beneficial to you because this format is scalable: you can change the size.

Other file formats—such as JPEG, TIFF, and GIF—are *bitmap* images. A bitmap image, also known as *pixel* art or *raster* art, is composed entirely of tiny squares of color called *pixels*. These pixels are arranged sequentially on an imaginary grid. If you enlarged a bitmap image, you would eventually see those little squares. So, when you make a bitmap picture larger than its original size, it looks a little fuzzy or grainy, because PowerPoint is "filling in" the missing squares of color.

A WMF is a vector image. It's created with a mathematical formula. A WMF keeps its quality and clarity whether you scale it to 400% or 40% of its original size. Another benefit of a WMF is that you can edit the image in PowerPoint.

> **Key Term**
>
> **GIF** Graphics Interchange Format, a bit-mapped graphics file format. GIF—pronounced "jiff" or "giff" (hard *g*)—supports color and various resolutions and includes data compression, which makes it especially suited for scanned photos.
>
> **WMF** Windows Metafile Format, a graphics file format used to exchange graphics information among Microsoft Windows applications. WMF files can hold vector images and bitmapped images.

Bitmap A means of representing a graphic image consisting of rows and columns of dots, with the value of each dot (whether filled or not) stored in one or more bits of data. The more bits used to represent a dot, the more colors and shades of gray that can be represented. Bit-mapped graphics are often referred to as *raster graphics*. Also *bit map*.

Vector image A graphic represented through geometrical formulas, rather than through patterns of dots (bitmaps). Vector-oriented images are more flexible than bit maps because they can be resized and stretched. Also known as *object-oriented graphics*.

Pixel The smallest element of an image. ("Pixel" is short for "picture element.") Every pixel is based on three smaller pixels—red, green, and blue, with the intensity of each color ranging from 0 to 255. The more pixels in an image, the greater the detail of the image. Once the resolution (number of pixels) is set, the detail cannot be increased.

Manipulating Clip Art

Once you've brought your piece of clip art (WMF format) into PowerPoint, you can pull it apart, recolor it, or manipulate it in the same way that PowerPoint will allow you to manipulate symbols.

If you simply want to recolor a portion or all of your clip art, single-click to select the piece of clip art, then right-click and select Format Picture from the pop-up menu. In the Format Picture pop-up window, select the Picture tab and click the recolor button at the bottom of the window. This will bring up the Recolor Picture pop-up window. You'll see all of the colors in that piece of clip art to the left and a thumbnail of the clip art on the right. Click any of the down arrows to the right of the color you want to change and select a new color. The thumbnail will automatically be updated with that new color. You may also click the Preview button to see the color change on the piece of clip art in the presentation. Once you've finished recoloring your clip art, click two OK buttons and your clip art colors are changed.

If you plan to manipulate the clip art in any other way, do not go through this step. First, ungroup the clip art. Select your piece of clip art, then click Draw on the Draw Toolbar and click Ungroup. A message will appear asking you to confirm that you

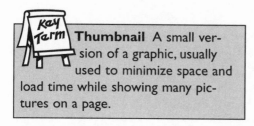

Thumbnail A small version of a graphic, usually used to minimize space and load time while showing many pictures on a page.

want to ungroup this piece of clip art. If so, and if the license agreement says it's OK, then click OK. You need to go back to this Ungroup function several times until the word "Ungroup" is grayed out. This means you can't ungroup this image any further.

Your piece of clip art has now been converted into many symbols. So, you can fill any of them with any color, gradient, texture, pattern, or picture. You can also delete parts of the clip art that you don't need.

When you're finished, select the entire piece of clip art by drawing your invisible rectangle around it (see Chapter 4), go to Draw Toolbar, and select Draw and Group. Now, your clip art is back to one piece.

Photos

Using photographs adds a sense of realism. Photos are a more accurate representation of your message or meaning. Although PowerPoint can read many file formats for photos, the main format you should use for photos is JPEG (.jpg). JPEGs will give you the quality you need for electronic presentations while keeping the file size down.

Here are some things to remember when using images:

- Make sure the file is a JPEG.
- You need only low-resolution (72 dpi) images for electronic presentations.
- Import images that are approximately the exact size as you want in your presentation.

As we said before, JPEGs are *bitmap* images, made of tiny squares of color. When you scale a photo up or down by more than 10%, you'll lose some quality. Why? Because PowerPoint has to fill in the blanks when you scale up or to decide what part of the image to delete when you scale down. PowerPoint doesn't do this well, so you should use a photo-editing software package if you want to scale up or down. Take the image into Microsoft Photo Editor or Adobe Elements (see Chapter 5) to manipulate it. Then import it into PowerPoint.

PowerPoint gives you limited control over your photos through the Picture Toolbar. Here's what you can do with the toolbar. The first icon on the left allows you to import a photo. The second icon, Image Control, allows you to change the image to grayscale, black and white, or watermark. The third and fourth icons change the photo's contrast. The fifth and sixth icons change the photo's brightness. The seventh icon allows you to crop the photo. (Don't be fooled: if you bring in a large image and crop off part of it, it will not reduce the image's file size. PowerPoint remembers the image as it was brought in and it keeps the original file size with it!) The eighth icon is the line style around the photo. The ninth icon will allow

> **Watermark** A translucent image. It's generally used behind text, but it can also be used as an overlay, such as for creating bar charts in front of graphics.

you to recolor vector images. (You can't use it for bitmaps.) The tenth icon opens the Format Picture pop-up window, which handles all of the controls on the toolbar. The eleventh icon allows you to set make one color in your photo transparent. (The color you want to set as transparent must be solid. For instance, if you have a white area around an image, the white must be consistent: if any part of that area is even slightly darker or lighter, then that section will not become transparent.) The twelfth icon resets the picture to its original format, as it was when you imported it. So, if you totally mess up your image with the other controls, don't worry. Click this icon and you can start all over!

Charts

Charts can be very effective if used properly. However, they can also become very complicated and even confuse and frustrate your audience. There are two basic points to keep in mind when creating charts:

Professional Photography

TOOLS Just like there are resources for clip art, there are also resources for stock photography. Here are some good sites to find photos:

- www.bizpresenter.com
- www.digitaljuice.com
- www.eyewire.com
- www.photodisc.com
- www.weststock.com

Use JPEGs at a low resolution—72 dpi. That is as high a resolution as a computer monitor can handle. The next best thing to JPEGs are TIFFs; you can open them up in Microsoft Photo Editor and do a Save As to change them to JPEGs. Again, check the license agreement to make sure it suits your needs. (You generally want to look for photos that are royalty-free.)

---

1. Use the right chart type.
2. Keep it simple.

One of the biggest problems with charts is when people use the wrong type of chart for their data. But it's really not difficult. To sum up our discussion in Chapter 4, there are basically three types of charts:

1. column or bar charts: for comparing values across categories
2. line or area charts: for displaying a trend over time or categories
3. pie charts: for showing contributions of values to a total

The second problem arises when people try to do too much—to show too much data, to plot too many points, to use too much glitz, and so on. Remember: you're using charts to represent your message graphically. If you make it too complicated, your audience won't grasp the message of the chart.

Here are four things to do to keep your charts simple:

1. Use 2-D charts instead of 3-D charts. Generally, the 3-D perspective tends to make the values of the elements in a chart a little confusing. Watch CNN. You won't see 3-D charts, because they try to keep it simple.

2. Use simple shapes to represent your data. PowerPoint now offers cones and pyramids to represent the data point. Generally, these shapes make it harder for the audience to clearly understand the exact value.
3. Plot only the important pieces of data to visually enhance your point.
4. Keep the data sheet hidden. Your audience will become over-whelmed if you expect them to try and see or read a data sheet next to the actual chart. If it's important for the audi-ence to see the raw data, then create a separate handout.

Sound

Sound can be a powerful tool—if used appropriately. But, unfor-tunately, it's often overused and improperly used.

Sound should be used only to draw attention to something or to enhance the presentation. Some good ways to use sound are as an opening or closing to the presentation, mouse-click-ing, and voice-over (e.g., testimonials from customers or an inspirational message from the CEO). Keep it professional: no typewriter noises on each letter, please!

Here's the basic rule: make sure your sound effects add impact. It's followed by a corollary: use sound effects sparingly.

Even the best sound effects tend to be less effective as you use them again and again. You may get a great reaction the first time, but by the fourth or fifth time you're likely to be getting annoyed expressions or yawns. These reactions are not good—unless the objective of your presentation is to show how sound effects can undermine a presentation.

PowerPoint allows you to import two sound file formats, WAV and MIDI. Most of your experience with sound will come in the form of WAV files.

Inserting Sounds

You can insert sounds in four ways:

- On a slide
- On the slide transition

Don't Be Gratuitous

Every time you're considering adding a sound to your presentation, think about the comment made by Jim Endicott in his article, "For Better Presentations, Avoid PowerPoint Pitfalls" (*Presentations*, June 1998): "The gratuitous use of any presentation effect is quickly identified by the audience for what it is: an attempt to hide low-impact content behind flashy technology."

- On an animation
- On an action

For sound on a slide: Go to Insert>Movies and Sounds>Sound from file. Locate the WAV file and click OK. You now have the sound on that slide.

For sound on the slide transition: Go to Slide Show>Slide Transition. The pop-up window shows an option to add sound.

It's as easy as that.

For sound on an animation: Single-click the object that you want the sound to be associated with, then select Slide Show> Custom Animation and the Effects tab. Click the down arrow where it says [No Sound] and you should see all of the sounds available through PowerPoint. You can also select Other Sounds... and locate a WAV file.

For sound on an action: You can use hyperlinks (actions) to add sound to your presentation. For example, you could use a WAV file of a mouse-click when you click on a button in your presentation. Single-click the button, then go to Slide Show>Action Settings. Make sure you're on the Mouse Click tab, then put a check in the Play sound box. Click the down arrow and locate your sound.

Tricks of the Trade

Value of Voice-Overs

The human voice provides a personalization that appeals to the emotional (right) side of the brain. It can complement the appeal of your information to the intellectual (left) side of the brain. By combining the approaches, you can both inform and persuade.

But the power of the voice can also work against you. If there's anything off with the pitch, intonation, or enunciation or the quality of the recording is inferior, the voice-over may undermine your presentation.

Using a Soundtrack

You can also play a song from a CD. Go to Insert>Movies and Sounds>Play CD Audio Track. It will bring up a pop-up menu. You have the option to Loop the sound, to select what tracks (sounds) you want to play through, and you can even be specific about the position in the song where you want to stop.

If you're going to distribute this presentation on CD, here's what you do. First, make sure any sounds that you'll insert are located in the same file as the presentation *before* you insert them into the presentation. Then, make sure that you put the sound on the CD in the same folder as the presentation.

Recording Narration

If you're going to create a self-running presentation, maybe to help your people learn about a new product or as a leave-behind for a meeting, you may want to use the Record Narration feature. In order to use this feature, you must have a microphone hooked up to your computer. (Most laptops come with a built-in microphone.)

Choose Slide Show>Record Narration. The first pop-up window allows you to set the quality of the sound. Click Settings (PowerPoint 97) or Change Quality (PowerPoint 2000). In the next pop-up window, select the down arrow in the Name field and choose CD Quality, then click OK.

You should be back at your Record Narration pop-up window. Notice that at the bottom it asks you if you want to link this file and where you want it to be placed after recording. Click the box and then make sure that the sound file is located in the same folder as the presentation for which you're recording this narration. Then, click OK.

Quality—A Sound Investment

Don't sacrifice quality. CD Quality is the highest preset quality. It also creates the largest file—about eight times the size of Radio Quality files, which are double the size of Telephone Quality files. But if you're putting this presentation on a CD, file size should not be an issue. Your presentations deserve the highest quality!

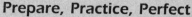

Prepare, Practice, Perfect

Smart Managing   Some people are naturally at ease and eloquent in front of a microphone; they never stammer or fumble for words or forget any points. Most people, however, are not that good. For them, it's smart to use a script, so the recording sounds more professional.

After you prepare your script, practice reading it until it seems natural. Mark up the script: underline the words that you want to emphasize, indicate pauses, and so forth. Then you can sound natural even if you're not a natural.

This will bring you to Slide Show Mode. Start talking! When you're done with that slide, advance to the next slide (use your mouse-click or Enter key) and start talking again. At any time, you can hit your Escape key on your keyboard and the recording will stop.

When you stop the recording, PowerPoint will ask you if you want to save the slide timings with the presentation. This means the show can be self-running and each slide will advance when you advanced during the narration. For example, if you talked for 10 seconds on the first slide, this slide will show for 10 seconds and then automatically go to the next slide.

Final Sound Bites

Generally, you want opening and closing music to play over only a few of slides or even just the first and last slide of a presentation. You want you music to work for you, not for you to work against your music.

Key Term   **Loop** Sound file played in its entirety over and over without stopping, rather than just once. It's basically a continual rewind and play. To stop the looping, you must advance (i.e., mouse-click or Enter key).

Here's the last word in our discussion of adding sounds to your presentation: keep the sounds simple and professional or you will distract the audience's attention away from the rest of your presentation.

Sound Tips

Here are some tips on using sound:

- If you insert the sound on the slide, there's an icon. Move the icon off the slide so it won't be seen.
- If you want a sound to play as soon as a slide appears, in Slide Show>Custom Animation select Automatically and enter 0 seconds.
- To play the sound over more than one slide, click the sound icon, then go to Slide Show>Custom Animation. In PowerPoint 97, you'll be on the Play Settings tab. In PowerPoint 2000, the tab is Multimedia Settings. Click the Continue slide show radial button if you want the show to continue while the music plays. Then, where it says Stop playing, click the After [ ] slides radial button and insert the number of slides for which you want the music to play. For example, to play the music for the next four slides, type 4 in the space. If you go to the More Options button, you can also choose to loop the music until you stop it.

Video

Video is probably the most accurate representation of your message. You can use it for such purposes as showing an off-site facility, providing a customer testimonial, delivering an executive message, demonstrating a procedure .... The list is endless.

The down side of video is the file size and some compatibility issues. But with a little knowledge and experience, you can avoid many problems.

Videos are compressed just like pictures. There are various formats, including AVI (Audio Video Interleave), MPEG (Moving Pictures Experts Group), and QuickTime. PowerPoint can show AVIs, MPEGs, and QuickTime movies. AVIs and MPEGs are the user-friendliest and easiest to find. To add QuickTime movies to a PC version of PowerPoint is no easy feat. You have to download the viewer for Windows and then, if you distribute this presentation, you have to make sure that the end user has this viewer. So, try to stick with the AVIs and MPEGs.

It's very easy to insert video into your presentation. Go to Insert>Movies and Sounds>Movie from File, then locate the

Keep It Short, Stupid!

Smart Managing   The infamous KISS strategy applies to using video in your presentations: Keep It Short, Stupid! Limit any clip to two minutes or so, at most, or you'll risk losing your audience. They may become bored or distracted—or so entranced that you'll have to fight to get them back.

movie and click OK. Single-click the video, then go to Slide Show>Custom Animation and you'll be on the Play Settings tab (PowerPoint 97) or the Multimedia Settings tab (PowerPoint 2000). You can do the same thing with video

clips as you did with audio clips. Also, make sure you select the More options button and click the rewind box.

The newest kid on the video block is Macromedia Flash movie (www.macromedia.com). You can use Flash to create movies and then import them into PowerPoint. You can save a Flash movie out as an AVI or you can save it out as a SWF (Shockwave Flash). The file is smaller if you use the native Flash format of SWF, but it's a little trickier to insert SWF files into PowerPoint.

TRICKS OF THE TRADE

Where Can I Get Video?

It's very easy to get VHS video converted to AVI or MPEG format. It's also not very expensive. Usually, a video-editing company can take your VHS video and convert it onto a CD for about $150. So, pull out that camcorder and start recording!

You can also purchase stock video for generic use. I think the best Web site out there is www.fourpalms.com. You can order and download online, the video is very inexpensive, and you can get it in multiple formats.

Here are the steps for putting a Flash movie in your PowerPoint presentation.

1. Write down the location of the Flash file or SWF file. (In my opinion, this first step is the most important.)
2. Choose View>Toolbars>Control Toolbox.
3. Click the button in the bottom right corner, More Controls (hammer and wrench).
4. Choose Shockwave Flash Object from the menu.
5. Drag the cursor (now crosshairs) and draw a box on your

screen. Don't make it the full size of the slide: PowerPoint
can't recognize any mouse-clicks on top of a Flash object.
Allow yourself some empty space to click to the next slide
in Slide Show view.

6. Right-click the box and choose Properties.
7. In the Properties window, click the top line, Custom. Then
   click the ellipsis at the right.
8. In the Property Pages dialog box, type the location of the
   SWF file that you wrote down in Step 1, including the file
   name and SWF extension.
9. Set the other parameters—for example, Quality: best or 1,
   Scale: ShowAll, WMode: Window.
10. Click Embed movie if you want to make sure it's always
    included with the PowerPoint presentation.
11. Click OK.
12. Close the Properties window using its close box.

Choose Slide Show view to see the movie. If your movie
doesn't appear in Normal view, it will appear when you return to
Normal view after running the slide show.

If the Flash movie doesn't play, open the Properties window
again and look at the Playing property. If it says False, click
Playing, then the down arrow and change the Playing property
to True. Files placed on Master will play continuously from slide
to slide to create an animated background. That effect can suit
your presentation, but it can also get distracting.

Ready, Set, No ...

Now your presentation should be in tiptop shape, with just the
right pizzazz from symbols, clip art, photos, charts, sound,
and/or video. So you're ready to move on? No.

It's always better to get at least a second opinion. Invite one
or several colleagues, friends, or family members to preview
your presentation. After all, you want to practice it at least once
anyway, right? So why not do it with an audience, even if only
of one?

Brief your "guinea pigs" on the purpose of your presentation and the background of your audience. Encourage them to be objective and critical. They can either ask questions and make comments as you go or take notes and save questions and comments until the end, as you like. Their reactions should help you get different perspectives on your creation and perhaps help you decide to make some changes in your presentation.

Then, you're ready to move on to the next chapter, where we focus on the setting of our meeting.

Manager's Checklist for Chapter 6

❏ There are many ways to add pizzazz to your presentation—symbols, clip art, photos, charts, sound, and video.

❏ Before you decide to add anything to your presentation for pizzazz, you ask yourself these two questions:

- Will this help my audience better understand my message?
- Will it match my presentation style?

❏ Don't limit yourself to the resources that come with PowerPoint. There are so many sources that you can tap to get just what you need.

❏ For every effect that you're considering, ask this basic question: Will this effect help my presentation achieve its objectives with this audience?

❏ Keep in mind the following guideline: "The gratuitous use of any presentation effect is quickly identified by the audience for what it is: an attempt to hide low-impact content behind flashy technology."

The Presentation Environment and Logistics

Until now, we've focused on the presentation itself. We've taken all the necessary steps toward creating our great presentation. We've done our research, designed our outline, created our presentation, and added pizzazz.

Now it's time to think about the presentation environment, the location where you and your hard work and all of your participants will come together. A good presenter will try to prepare and, if possible, control the logistics of the meeting at which you present:

- Date and time
- Room environment
- Equipment

Date and Time

If you have the authority or power, it's best to determine the right date and time for your meeting. Choosing the date and time gives you a little more control over the audience's frame of mind.

First, you want to try to select a date when over 95% of your participants will be available. You also want to make sure that key individuals are part of that 95%. This should be obvious.

Next, try not to have the meeting on Monday or Friday. On Monday, most people are getting back into the swing of things after their weekend. They may be busy getting organized and ready for another week or they may be enjoying weekend memories. On Friday, most people are winding down for the weekend, trying to complete tasks or projects, and making plans for the weekend. Meetings on either of these two days will not give you a very attentive audience, so try to schedule your meetings during the middle of the week.

Time also plays an important role in the success of your meeting. We're all well aware that right after lunch people tend to be lethargic, so try to avoid meetings during this time. Late afternoon meetings may also cause a conflict for you, because people are winding down for the day and may be distracted by the need for coffee or a snack. The best time for holding a meeting is in the morning. Try to let your participants have 30 minutes to get into the office and get situated. For instance, if your office hours begin at 8:30 a.m., then start your meeting at 9:00 a.m. Also, try to end your meetings about 30 minutes prior to the office's usual lunch break. This way your participants probably won't be focused yet on their lunch plans.

And what if the scheduling is beyond your control? Probably the best strategy is to schedule breaks. Studies have

A Matter of Timing

Smart Managing Although everybody seems to agree that it's bad to schedule meetings immediately after lunch, there's no consensus on good times for meetings. Some experts believe that 11 a.m. and 4 p.m. are the best times to schedule meetings, because participants will stay on task better right before going to lunch or leaving for home.

Timing depends to a great extent on the workplace, on location, practices, employee responsibilities, and culture. Part of knowing the people who will be attending your presentation is knowing how they work, which should allow you to determine the best timing.

shown that the average person can pay attention in a meeting for about 20 minutes before starting to fidget, daydream, or think about other things. If there's enough variety in your presentation, you can minimize the effects of this tendency. Even so, after about 90 minutes, it's likely that attention and participation will be deteriorating. If your meeting will run that long, you should schedule a 10-minute break. You should break earlier if your meeting is during the after-lunch lull. Be sure to let participants know at the start of a meeting that you've scheduled a break and give an approximate time. That will make it easier for them to focus on the meeting.

When you break, tell the participants exactly when you'll resume—and make it clear that you intend to keep to the schedule, out of respect for everyone. If you provide refreshments, avoid anything heavy or sugary, to minimize drowsiness. If you don't provide refreshments, allow enough time for participants to get something from the lunch area or vending machines. If they're unfamiliar with the site, tell them where they can find beverages and snacks—and phones, for those without cell phones. Finally, start the meeting at the scheduled time; don't wait for stragglers.

Room Environment

The environment of the room is also critical to the success of your meeting. It must be able to accommodate you and your audience comfortably. There are five keys to making sure the room is right for your meeting:

- Room size and setup
- Lighting
- Facilities
- Temperature
- Acoustics

We listed some of the questions to consider in Chapter 1, under "Place." Now, we'll move beyond the answers to those questions.

Room Size and Setup

Determining the proper setup of your room will help you determine the size needed. You should know how many people will be in your audience and you need to make sure that your room and setup accommodate them all comfortably and are appropriate to your presentation.

If you can select your room, make sure it fits your presentation. Are you giving a speech? Is your presentation interactive? Is it informal? The room size and setup can range from an auditorium setting to a conference room table. If there are chairs and tables, you have choices about ways to arrange them.

The number of participants will help determine how to set up the room. If the room holds 50 people and there will be 40-50 attending, you may want to set up the room classroom style. Classroom style allows for a room to hold the maximum amount of people. Work can be completed either via computer or handout.

For a more informal discussion, a U-shaped arrangement is best. This allows for dialogue and interaction between you and the participants as well as among the participants.

Unfortunately, we cannot always control our environment, so we must try to anticipate the environment. If you do many or all of your presentations on-site, familiarize yourself with the rooms that you'll be using. Then, you'll know how to prepare for each and, if you have the luxury of choosing a room, you'll know which one is appropriate for your specific presentation. The two styles that are used most in day-to-day presentations are classroom and conference room.

Classroom Style. Classroom style room setups are best suited for training sessions, seminars, or hands-on types of presentations. These room styles tend to be a little less formal and they allow you to present freely from anywhere in the room. The setup should provide a table at the front of the room for you and then rows of tables for the participants. There should be a center aisle and outside aisles so you can move easily around the room. Normally, the rows are parallel, but you can also

---

Tips for Classroom Settings

If you're setting up your room in classroom style, make sure
that each participant has enough space. Generally in a classroom setting, participants have handouts or are taking notes. Test the
space you are giving them. Do they have enough room to open the
handout without bothering the people on either side of them? Is there
enough room for their notepad? Is there enough "elbow room"? If
you're giving participants enough space to be comfortable, you'll make it
easier for them to pay attention and get the most out of the meeting.

---

angle the tables toward the center (chevron style) so participants can see better and to increase interaction.

Conference Room Style. You'll give many of your presentations
in conference rooms. This style is usually best for smaller groups.
The meeting can be formal or informal. In this style of setup, you
want to make sure that the presentation is visible from every
chair in the room. Generally, you want to keep the chairs farther
away from the front, so you don't block the view for anyone.
Also, make sure that your AV equipment is not too high or obtru-
sive to anyone in the room. Try to allow enough space between
the chairs so participants have room to take notes.

Facilities

No matter what type of setup you use, you must make sure that
your room is properly equipped for your presentation needs.
Even if you've asked the questions listed in Chapter 1, always
try to personally check the room before you present. If you're
presenting at on off-site location, confirm with your con-

Yes, They're Adults, but ....

The people who attend your presentation are adults and
should be responsible for preparing for the event. However,
sometimes even adults forget to bring along a pad of paper and a pen.
Some facilities provide paper and pens for each participant. You might
not want to do this, but it makes sense to bring several pads of paper
and a few pens to lend out to participants who somehow forget. They'll
appreciate your kindness and they'll get more out of your presentation.

tact person the room will have everything you need. Here are some questions to consider:

- Is the outlet conveniently located or do you need an extension cord?
- Is there a screen or will you be projecting on a wall?
- Do you need a phone jack or multiple power supply?
- If you need speakers, are there already some in the room or should you bring your own?

Again, checking on the facility and being prepared will help your presentation run smoothly.

Minimize Disruptions

One of the most important items in the facility may actually be *outside*. If you're serious about avoiding distractions, you should make sure that Do Not Disturb signs are posted outside the doors, with a pocket or a bulletin board for messages for participants.

Lighting

The lighting in the room is also critical to your presentation. Often, conference rooms or hotel meeting spaces are equipped with fluorescent lighting. The best type of lighting to have is usually set up on a grid or in a pattern. This is helpful when you're projecting, so you can turn down the lights that shine on the screen. Turning down the lights only in the front of the room helps your audience to see the screen better and allows enough light for them to take notes or read along with a handout. Make sure to turn the lights back up during breaks or Q&A periods.

Make sure you know where the light controls are. If they're located where you can't access them easily, try to assign a helper who's close to them—preferably not a member of your audience. Also, be prepared that the front of the room might be too dark for you to see your notes. If this is the case, bring a small light that you can set up, similar to a podium light.

Temperature

The temperature of the room will impact the mood and level of engagement of your participants. If the room is not comfortable,

> ## Using the Right Background Color ⚠️ CAUTION!
> The lighting in your room can tremendously impact your presentation. Try to determine the lighting condition of the room *before* you select a background color. If you can control the lighting in the room and you can fade the lights on the screen, then go with light text against a darker background color. If you cannot control the lighting or there are a lot of windows in the room, then go with dark text against a lighter background color. Too much light in the room will fade out darker backgrounds and you will not have a good contrast.

they'll be focused on the temperature, not your presentation. If you have a large room or auditorium, try to make it cool before the meeting begins; the temperature will rise when it fills up. If the room is small, like a conference room, keep the temperature moderate. If you cannot control the temperature of the room, make sure that you know how to contact someone who can change it for you. And be ready to adjust the setting if the temperature changes during the presentation.

What if you can't get the temperature right? Don't ignore the problem. Acknowledge that it's uncomfortable for the participants, apologize, and encourage them to make the best of it. Showing that you're concerned about their comfort will likely improve the situation. In fact, sometimes a shared problem brings people together, creating a sense of community—"we're all in the same boat."

Acoustics

If your audience can't hear you well enough, then your presentation is worthless. The message is not getting across and the participants become frustrated. If they start asking each other what you're saying, the situation deteriorates rapidly.

Knowing the acoustics of your room is especially important in larger rooms. Your voice needs to be loud enough for everyone to hear. If you know that you're a "soft talker" or "low talker," a wireless lavaliere microphone is your best bet. Adjust the level of your microphone before your presentation. After you introduce yourself, ask if the people in the back of the room can hear you OK. That way, you don't need to guess and you show your audience you care.

In smaller rooms, make sure that you're not blowing your audience away. You don't want too much sound or an echo in the room. Test how your voice projects and how the presentation audio comes through *before* the presentation.

⚠️ CAUTION!

Sudden Sounds

You've checked out the acoustics of your facility and they're great. Then, you do your presentation and everybody can hear clearly ... every time a cell phone rings or a pager beeps.

To avoid that scenario, you should ask participants to set their phones and pagers to vibrate or turn them off. Then, remind them of the scheduled break, so they know when they can resume contact with the outside world.

Equipment

It's essential to your presentation to have the right equipment—and a backup plan. Technology has brought us a long way, but it can also set us back if we're not prepared.

We've all heard the horror stories about laptops crashing and projectors not being compatible with our equipment. The key here is to be prepared. It's best if you can bring your own equipment. Then you know it's compatible and it works. If you're using other equipment, test it before the meeting.

Here are some questions to consider while checking out the equipment:

- Is my laptop compatible with the projector?
- Do I have all the necessary cables, including sound (if needed)?
- Does the presentation project properly?
- Do my presentation colors look the same on the screen as on your laptop?
- Is the presentation contrast still good?
- Is the projected image bright enough?
- Does the projector have two computer ports (if needed)?

- Does the projector have a video port (if needed)?
- Can I plug my laptop into a power supply?
- Is the projector at the right distance from the screen?
- Do I have a contact name in case of emergency?

All projectors are created different, so testing is the key.

Try to be prepared for the worst. If you bring your own projector, bring an extra bulb. Always have a backup of your presentation on 3.5 disk or CD-ROM. (Avoid using a medium that most people don't have, such as a Zip disk.) The most important thing to remember about equipment is to test it before you use it.

Questions for Presenters

> ### Researching Projection Equipment
> **TRICKS OF THE TRADE**
>
> If you're in the market for a new projector, but you don't know where to begin, go to the *Presentations* Web site, www.presentations.com. The editors of this industry publication are always reviewing the latest presentation equipment. They provide unbiased reviews of projectors, digital cameras, software, etc. There are also helpful articles on presenting and presentation design.

Here is a list of questions you should ask yourself before any meeting:

Did I test the equipment? Make sure everything you need is there and works at least 30 minutes prior to the beginning of the meeting.

Is the room set up properly for my meeting? If not, you may have to rearrange it before the meeting. You may also need to change the seating if fewer people show up than anticipated.

Can I control the lighting? Always test the lighting with the presentation projected. If there are windows, close the blinds before participants arrive.

Is the room temperature satisfactory? Keep it moderate and not too warm. Have the contact person's information handy before you begin.

Does everyone know where the restrooms are? If you're at an off-site facility, familiarize the audience with the facility at the beginning of the meeting.

Will I have enough handouts? Bring extra handouts; it's better to have 10 left over than to come up one or two short.

Do I have a backup disk of my presentation? Make sure it is in a universal format. If you're presenting off-site, you may also want to have transparencies handy.

Do I have water available? Always have water on hand. Room temperature water is better than cold or ice water. Cold water constricts the throat, making it uncomfortable to speak easily. (Some folks recommend a dash of lemon juice, to help keep the throat clear.) Although hot tea is good because of the temperature, you should avoid tea that contains caffeine and/or tannin, as both of these restrict the throat.

Do I need any other visual support? You may want to have a flip chart or white board and with markers available to help you change the flow of your presentation.

Do I have a clock easily visible or watch to keep next to the computer? Make sure you stay on time during your presentation.

Have I scheduled enough breaks? Allow for breaks, not just for your participants but also for yourself—especially if there's no one helping you facilitate an off-site meeting. During the breaks, you can use the restroom, make sure snacks and beverages are stocked, adjust the room temperature, and answer questions that took up too much time during the presentation.

Asking yourself these questions can help you ensure that your presentation will go as smoothly as possible and be optimally prepared for the unexpected.

Manager's Checklist for Chapter 7

❏ Know as much as possible about the facility for your presentation, prepare for that setting, and control the logistics.

❏ Choose the date and time for your meeting carefully, if you have the authority or power. If not, know what to expect of your participants and how to offset the negative effects of distractions, preoccupations, and moods.

❏ Setting is critical to the success of a meeting. There are five keys to making sure the setting is right: room size and setup, lighting, facilities, temperature, and acoustics.

❏ It's essential to have the right equipment, to check out all of the equipment, and to have a backup plan. If possible, bring your own equipment. If not, test the equipment in advance.

❏ Develop a checklist of questions to answer about every presentation—and then use it.

Presenter's Guide
to Facilitation

Start Right

You and your presentation might be 100% ready to go, but if you haven't fully thought through your opening, your well-prepared presentation may not have the impact you want.

Use the opening of the meeting to set the pace. As the presenter, you're responsible for getting things started in the right direction with the right level of energy. It's critical to engage your participants from the beginning.

Breaking the Ice

Presenters will often use an icebreaker to get a meeting started. Most people think of an icebreaker as being useful only for a meeting when the participants are unfamiliar with each other. Although that's when an icebreaker can be crucial, it's not the only occasion for using one. In meetings when everyone knows one another, you can benefit from an icebreaker to pull participants away from their separate worlds into a community and set the tone for the meeting.

To do that, try using one of these icebreaker exercises:

> **Facilitate** To make easier or less difficult. That definition from the dictionary, simple and straightforward, should guide you as a facilitator. Focus on your goals; whatever you can do to make it easier or less difficult for your participants to achieve those goals is effective facilitation.

- **Pre-test.** Administer a simple 10-question test on what will be covered in the meeting, score it, and then review it at the close of the meeting to help show participants what they've learned. Remember: people don't know what they don't know.

- **Catch the liar.** People introduce themselves, one by one, telling three things about themselves. One of the three things is to be a lie. The others try to determine which one is the lie. Then at the end, they all vote on the most creative or successful liar.

> **Icebreakers**
> What icebreakers have worked for other presenters? You can get some good ideas from these two books:
> - *Games Trainers Play*, by John W. Newstrom and Edward E. Scannell (McGraw-Hill, 1989)
> - *100 Training Games*, by Gary Kroehnert (McGraw-Hill, 1992)

- **"Who am I?"** As participants arrive at the meeting, give each a nametag with the name of a famous person to put on his or her back. The "celebrities" then circulate to ask questions of each other in order to figure out whose name they're wearing.

Take a moment to think about the last time you were really impressed when meeting someone. Now think: what did that person do to make this impression? Starting a presentation or meeting out right is just like making a great first impression: you only have one chance.

To decide whether you should use a particular icebreaking activity, ask yourself these six questions:

1. Will it help us progress toward the main objective of my presentation?
2. Will it get every participant involved?
3. Will it encourage the participants to get (better) acquainted and feel more comfortable together?
4. Is it simple enough to explain, set up, and carry out?
5. Is it appropriate for the number of participants and the setting?
6. Do we have enough time for it?

It's up to You

The key to using icebreakers is for you to be prepared, feel comfortable, and seem confident with the activity. Even the best activity can fail if you don't seem ready for it—and sometimes an activity will succeed primarily because of the style and skill of the facilitator.

As you prepare your next presentation, take some time and use this information to determine how to use an icebreaker to make a great first impression. With a good icebreaker, you and your participants will not only get more out of the meeting, but also have a lot of fun.

Keep Participants Engaged in Your Presentation

Now that you've gotten everyone's attention, you need to think about how to keep the energy going. No one said presenting was easy. It can be one of the most draining activities you will experience. In fact, if it's not, you may not be putting all that you should into your presentations!

Keeping an eye on the level of engagement can be tricky, but it's very important. There are several techniques (like icebreakers) to help get the participants engaged and keep them there—but you're not likely to think to use them if you're not picking up on a potential lack of engagement.

Many times your personal "radar" will pick up on the fact that you may be losing people. When this happens, don't second-guess your instincts—react!

However, your radar will not catch everything. So, rather than relying on it to detect when you're losing people, include checkpoints in your presentation. These could be in the form of slides or simply notes on your personal agenda.

Here are some ideas for keeping participants engaged in your presentation:

1. Do the participants understand the information?
   - Ask two or three questions to verify understanding. This shouldn't take more than two minutes. You could put the questions on a slide or just ask them orally.
   - Have a participant recap a section that has just been covered. Ask for a volunteer first, so as not to embarrass anyone. Help the volunteer if he or she gets stuck and, if need be, get others to jump in and help.

2. Do the participants understand why this information is important to them?
   - In Chapter 2, I mentioned the radio station WII-FM, whose call letters stand for "What's in it for me?" In many cases, people must get an answer to that question before they'll engage. So ask participants to comment on what they're getting out of the presentation. Also, ask them what they'll gain by using the information presented thus far.

3. How are you doing in terms of your agenda? Are you on track with time goals you've set?
   - Some participants will watch the clock and check the agenda. If you're running behind, they may worry about other things they need to do and how their schedules may be affected. Those thoughts distract them. If you're off track and you need time to regroup, take a quick break. Then tell the participants how you plan to cover the information necessary and end on time. If it's impossible to finish in the allotted time, allow a break so they can make any needed arrangements.

Another way to verify that participants are engaged is to check in with the participants during breaks and lunch to see what they're getting out of the meeting. If this is a meeting with your subordinates, breaks are a great time to chat with them to check their level of understanding and retention.

Participants may also approach you between sessions and want to know if you have a few minutes after the meeting to talk. If you have time right then, don't wait; take them aside immediately and find out what's on their minds. If they have questions or concerns, they're less likely to be fully engaged in your presentation. Even if you just listen to them and promise to get back with them later to finish the discussion, they'll have it off their minds. Also, try to prepare them (and yourself) for the rest of the session. Mention some of the points to come and get them thinking in that direction.

Ways to Deal with Difficulties

You need to stay engaged with the group. After you've worked through some of these points with the participants, think about any changes you might need to make. If the presentation is not going the way you want it to go, extend the break to give yourself time to rework the agenda. Yes, it's your meeting and you should be allowed to set the pace and change the information to be covered, but if it's not working as you had planned, why push it?

To be a good presenter, you must have the ability to think on your feet, to adapt, to overcome any obstacles that get in your way. Think about making popcorn. Do all of the kernels pop at the same time? No. It's the same with the people participating in your presentation. They won't all be getting it at the same time, so checking on their understanding is critical to the success of your presentation. Think through the rest of the agenda, then decide if you need to make a change in the pace or direction of the meeting.

Changing the Direction of the Presentation

Depending on how your participants are doing with the presentation, you may need to change the content or the direction.

If you feel that what you're trying to communicate is not sinking in, add more examples or stop the presentation and work through a real-life situation. You should always be prepared for this eventuality and have plenty of examples and situations ready to go.

Here are two examples:

- You're working through a sales plan on a new product and the participants are having trouble understanding or buying into the sales targets. But you're ready to refer to an existing product and show how it was rolled out and how the actual sales compared with the projected sales of that product when it first came out.
- You're presenting some marketing ideas for a mature product line and you realize that your ideas are not winning over the participants. But you're ready to cite success stories of mature products that have enjoyed renewed sales when marketed differently.

You may not need your contingency examples and situations, but you're ready just in case. And it's always better to plan too much than to plan too little.

Different Strokes for Different Folks

It's important to take various approaches in a presentation. In a perfect environment, a presentation would both impart a lot of information and be interactive. Whenever you can get participants to take an active part in the presentation instead of just listening and watching, their level of understanding and engagement will increase dramatically.

You know from experience that we all learn in different ways. Some people learn best by watching, some by reading, some by listening, and others would rather jump right in and do

Visual, Auditory, and Kinesthetic

TRICKS OF THE TRADE A commonly accepted theory categorizes learning styles as *visual*, *auditory*, and *kinesthetic*. We all learn in all three ways, but one tends to dominate.

Visual participants learn best when they see, such as with graphs, pictures, and written text.

Auditory participants learn best when they hear, such as through the usual oral presentation.

Kinesthetic participants learn best they do things, when motion and touch are involved, such as with role-plays and other interactive activities.

it. So, if you combine text, graphics, script, and interactivity in your presentation, you're most likely to reach your participants and help them all get the most out of the experience.

Consider the different ways that people learn to drive a manual transmission car. Some will want to hear the instructor talk about how the transmission works and watch him or her shift the gears. Others might need to read the explanation of the gear pattern in the manual. Still others would go crazy if they had to wait that long to get behind the wheel and try it themselves. They just want the keys and a chance to figure it out.

That's why most corporate training programs have several different components to them—operational/procedural manuals, videos, tests, and "hands on." This is how you should lay out your presentations.

The most important point to remember is that it's very hard for people to change how they perceive and process. If you want to reach people with your presentations, you should take responsibility for being sensitive to the learning styles of your participants. The best way to accomplish this is to make sure, whenever possible, that there's a little something for everyone. Create a handout. Provide whatever kinds of "hands-on" you can. Even if it's only a small part of the whole presentation, do what you can to engage your participants in various ways.

Think One by One

Of growing interest in education and training is the subject of **Smart**
learning styles and multiple intelligences. There are so many **Managing**
theories out there and each one has generated at least one book, so we
could hardly do any of them justice here.

But what a smart manager can learn from all of the discussion and
experiments is that individuals perceive and process experiences in
different ways. So, when you're preparing your presentation, try to
think of it from the various perspectives of people you know—friends,
family members, neighbors. How would each of them react to it? What
could you do to make it work better with each? That type of diver-
gent thinking can help you present in ways that help all participants get
more out of your presentations.

How to Handle Tough Situations

There will be times when situations will come up that distract
from the flow or objective of your presentation. No matter what
you do, it will happen. The true test of your preparation and
people skills is how you handle these situations.

Four Situations and Ways to Handle Them

Problem: Know-it-all—A participant who feels like more of an
expert than you.
Solution: Don't fight it! Involve know-it-alls in your presentation.
They may have some great information to contribute. Allowing
them to participate and share their thoughts will not only show
the other participants how confident you are, but also help them
get more out of your presentation.
Example: Sometimes, your participants may not be all at the
same levels of knowledge. You have to size this up at the beginning of the presentation, then aim at the level of most of the
participants. There will always be someone there who knows
more about at least some aspect of the topic than most, perhaps even more than you—and sometimes that person will feel
like showing off that knowledge.

Problem: Unprepared participants—Those who haven't prepared for the presentation as you requested

Solution: Be flexible! You may need to take something out of your agenda to allow the group time to get up to speed. Keep in mind your overall objective of the presentation. Don't try to force your agenda; modify it to meet your objective.

Example: During a P&L presentation, you find that not all of the participants brought what they need. Your main objective is to make sure they're planning properly. You decide you can still do this by going about it a different way. Change from your original plan of having individuals review their P&Ls to having the participants form small groups to review one member's P&Ls. Don't let the fact that some people are not prepared affect what you've set out to do in this meeting.

Problem: After-lunch nap time—One of the toughest times to keep people engaged

Solution: If you have anything to do with planning the lunch selections, go light—and no heavy desserts. If not, then adjust your presentation. Take shorter breaks more often. If you really need to get everyone going again, get out those icebreakers.

Example: You see that shortly after lunch some heads are starting to bob. Quickly check your agenda and maybe switch things around to get into a subject that might be more interactive. If need be, get participants up out of their chairs to do an activity. (It's always good to have one ready if you're scheduled for early afternoon.) Remember: you must remain flexible; it's your responsibility to keep them engaged.

Problem: Non-stop talker—A participant who carries on conversations during the presentation

Solution: This can be very difficult if you're from outside the company or from another department in the company. In either of these situations, avoid causing the person to get defensive. He or she may just have a better understanding of what you're presenting or not be challenged enough by it. On the next break, ask the person for feedback. As you resume after the break, mention that you were talking to ___ (use the name of

---

Facilitator vs. Expert

Smart Managing

A good facilitator is a step beyond an expert. A facilitator not only knows the topic well—he or she must know more about the topic than most of the participants—but also feels confident in his or her presentation skills. As facilitator, you create the environment for transfer of knowledge, whether the knowledge comes from you or from others in the meeting. The environment you create encourages participation, so participants can learn from each other.

An expert may know almost every detail about a topic, but knowledge doesn't necessarily qualify an expert as a great presenter. When you find yourself face to face with an expert in your group, use him or her as an ally, not an enemy. In some cases, you may have to swallow a little pride, but if it helps you meet your overall objectives of the meeting, it's worth the extra efforts.

---

the person), who had some good points about what you've covered thus far in the presentation. Take a few moments to share what you talked about. This usually makes the talker feel more involved and want to stay engaged and participate with you instead of others. Of course, it's possible that putting the spotlight on this person might cause him or her to disrupt the meeting even more. If that happens, don't hesitate to go to the leader of the group and ask for help in controlling the individual.

If you're giving the presentation to people who report to you, obviously you can handle the situation much differently. On the next break (or you may even call an unscheduled break), take the person aside and ask him or her to get the talking under control. If the person claims to already know what you're presenting, explain that others do not and that if he or she continues to disrupt that learning opportunity you'll ask the person to leave and then deal with him or her later. As I've stated several times already, it's your responsibility to present the information so that the group gets it. Don't let a disruptive participant get in the way of that objective.

Going Beyond Your Presentation

How fast do we forget what's been presented to us? Within the first 24 hours, we lose 75% of what we just learned if we don't use it in some way.

Encourage the participants to take what they've learned to someone else. Will they remember everything you said? No. However, even if they repeat only half of it, more will stay with them than if they did nothing with the information at all.

How long does it take to change a habit? At least 21 days, according to behavioral psychologists. Many times people give up too soon. They try to do something with what they've learned at a meeting, but after a few days it still seems too hard to make the change stick, so they give up.

Challenge your participants to take one or two things from the information they've received from you and set goals for integrating change into their habits. The goals can be personal and/or professional. Tell them to try for 21 days and to stay disciplined and honest with themselves. Then, tell them that if they do so and still can't make the desired change they should call you for further advice and coaching. Nine times out of 10, if they call and you ask them how they executed the 21-day plan, you'll find gaps that they should close as they attack the plan again.

Here are two more ways to make the new information stick:

- Prepare a challenge or specific task to help the participants retain and/or use this information.
- Challenge the participants to spend a few moments during the close of the meeting to write out a short list of things to do as they try to use what they've just learned.

Manager's Checklist for Chapter 8

❑ It's critical to engage your participants from the beginning and get things started in the right direction with the right level of energy.

❑ Be attentive to the reactions of your participants and ready to check for comprehension, take a break, and/or change direction, according to the situation.

❑ Since we all perceive and process in different ways, your presentation will be more effective if you use several ways to present information and make your points.

❑ Participants will not always come prepared, pay attention, and not disrupt the presentation. The true test of your preparation and people skills is how you handle these situations.

❑ Prepare some suggestions or activities to help your participants use and retain what they get out of your presentation.

Getting Ready and Delivering Your Presentation

You've done everything to properly prepare for your presentation. You've done your research, you've got great slides, you think you have a pretty good idea about what your audience expects. Now you are going to actually deliver the goods. Here's where you put it all together. To make sure all your preparation pays off, this chapter will help you give a great presentation.

Butterflies

The first point to cover in this chapter, and often the first point in any book about public speaking, is those legendary butterflies that swarm around in our stomachs as we get up in front of a crowd—or sometimes even just think about doing so. Whether you call it butterflies, stage fright, or whatever, it's fear.

This fear is perfectly normal—but that's probably not much consolation when those butterflies start churning. What can you do to reduce or eliminate that fear? You start by understanding it.

Daria Price Bowman, author of the book *Presentations* (Adams, 1998), defines it as "the fear of the unknown in a situation over which you may have no control." So, to conquer that fear, you work to minimize the unknown and maximize your control. Here are some suggestions to help you do just that.

In advance of your presentation:

- Practice—a lot. Don't just think your presentation through: act it out, in front of friends, family, or colleagues. Time each section of your presentation and develop a schedule.
- Memorize the first two minutes of your presentation, so you breeze on through the time when the butterflies are most active. But don't try to memorize your entire presentation: then it won't seem as natural and you'll worry over forgetting your lines. (If you feel better memorizing something, memorize the organization and the key points and concepts of your presentation.)
- Develop notes, either on index cards or on sheets of paper. (More on this later.)
- Get enough sleep, especially the night before you're making your presentation.

In the hours before you present:

> ### "I Don't Need to Practice"
>
> If that's what you're thinking, think again. Practice is what people do so when they get to the real thing—whether a presentation, a performance, or a sporting event—they get it right. Even if you don't have much time, use it to run through what you want to say and how you want to say it. Even a little practice is better than none. It's great insurance against stumbling over your words and making sure things go the way you hope they will.

- Think positive thoughts: visualize yourself feeling at ease with the audience.
- Use affirmation (e.g., "I've got something they need or want" or "I can do this. I'm prepared. It will all go well.").
- Eat light.
- Avoid coffee and alcohol.
- Make sure all the equipment is working properly.

- Remember that the people in your audience are human, too, just like you. They want you to succeed.

When you enter the room:

- Focus on making your movements fluid and confident, neither too slow nor too fast.
- Find a few friendly faces in the audience, for reassurance.
- Smile. Show that you want to be there.
- Be yourself.

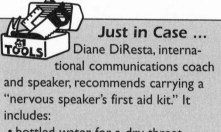

Just in Case ...
Diane DiResta, international communications coach and speaker, recommends carrying a "nervous speaker's first aid kit." It includes:
- bottled water for a dry throat
- lozenges for a sore throat
- B vitamins to reduce stress
- soothing herbal tea to relax
- tape or CD player with relaxing music

In earlier chapters, we've emphasized the importance of preparation—of planning your presentation, of preparing your slides and handouts, of knowing as much as possible about the people and place. If you plan, you minimize problems. If you anticipate potential problems, you can virtually eliminate them.

This includes being prepared for the effects of fear. If you make a mistake at the beginning, don't be afraid to just start again. If something happens later, simply apologize. It's no big deal unless you let it become big.

Most presenters become less nervous with experience—or at least better at overcoming it. When we're nervous, it's rarely as obvious to others as we think it is. Your audience will not notice the small changes in your voice or any little mistakes; if you remember that fact, you're more likely to appear calm and confident.

One last thing: don't expect to get rid of those butterflies. The best public speakers, people who seem so relaxed in front of crowds, still feel the fear. But they use it to their advantage, turning that nervous energy into a dynamic presence. And what works for them can work for you.

Before You Begin

Words of Wisdom
Actor Jack Lemmon once noted in a TV interview, "Failure seldom stops you. What stops you is the fear of failure." Good words to keep in mind!

There are a number of things to think about to make sure you're ready to deliver a successful presentation. Things to think about and to help you prepare include your clothes, your voice and speaking style, and some ways to warm up effectively.

Appearance

We all know those sayings, "Clothes make the man/woman" and "Dress for success." Appearances are important in a presentation. The members of the audience are judging you by your appearances from the very start. So dress comfortably, but appropriately. What does that mean?

If you know your audience, you should have a good idea of what their expectations are. How do the members of your audience dress for work? What's the culture of their workplace? What's their image? If you project the wrong image, you can undermine your credibility. You want meet their expectations for appearance just as you want to focus your presentation to meet their expectations for content.

Voice

Another aspect of appearance, in a way, is your voice. Your voice is the clothing in which you dress your words. Just as your clothing sends messages

Be Conservative
Smart Managing
A good rule is to dress just a little more formally than your audience. You don't want your appearance to distract from what you want to say. Also, it's not just a matter of dressing appropriately for the circumstances. You should also choose clothes in which you feel good about yourself, so you come across as comfortable and confident.

as soon as the audience sees you, your voice sends messages as soon as the audience hears you. It may be a good idea to record your voice to see how it comes across to others. Try to sound natural, so your rhythm and tone is appropriate to the message you're delivering.

Here are a few negative voice qualities that you should work to reduce or eliminate:

- high pitch
- nasality
- strong accent
- hoarseness

Some of us have great voices by nature. Others may never be able to get rid of negative characteristics. But whatever the particular features of your voice, you can work to develop four important qualities—volume, pitch, intonation, and enunciation.

Volume is relatively easy to regulate. Speak loudly enough to reach all the members of your audience without overpowering those closest to you. If you're unsure whether you're reaching everyone, you can simply ask if they all can hear you well enough. You can also read their body language: if people are leaning forward or cupping their ears or furrowing their brows, it may mean that you're not getting through to them. As for the people who may be feeling overpowered by your volume, you can often read the discomfort on their faces or by the way they shift around uncomfortably as you speak.

Maybe you detect problems with your volume at the beginning of your presentation, but you can't do anything to resolve the problem, particularly if the layout of the room or the acoustics make it impossible. In that case, just stop, apologize for the problem, and suggest that participants change their seats if your voice will be too strong or too weak.

Volume also serves to emphasize key points and draw attention to your message. Sometimes getting a little louder or dropping your voice to a whisper can add a dramatic effect to your words. However, make sure that you don't use the effects of volume too often.

Pitch can be more difficult to control. To find your optimum pitch, the pitch that will be easiest on your voice and on your

---

The Right Emphasis

Diane DiResta, in her book *Knockout Presentations* (Chandler House Press, 1998) suggests practicing intonation by reading the following sentences and emphasizing the italicized word to change the meaning:

I didn't say you stole money.
I *didn't* say you stole money.
I didn't *say* you stole money.
I didn't say *you* stole money.
I didn't say you *stole* money
.I didn't say you stole *money*.

---

audiences, use the "uh huh" technique. Say "uh huh" a few times. Professionals have discovered that the pitch you use to hum "uh huh" is probably the one that will be most comfortable to you and to your audience.

Intonation takes a little more practice to improve. Some people tend to speak in a monotone, especially with a crowd. You want to put more feeling into your voice, to make it livelier, by changes in your intonation. And you want your intonation to support your words: accentuate the key words, the nouns and verbs that carry the weight of your message.

You also want to avoid patterns that contribute nothing to your words, intonations that can distract, annoy, or lull. (Sometimes you can pick up on these intonations on the local TV news, when a reporter tends to stress every fifth or seventh syllable, for example, regardless of the word and whether it merits the emphasis.)

Enunciation is both easiest and hardest to improve. It's easy, because we can all enunciate better if we focus on it. It's hard, because we've got to focus consistently, until it becomes natural. Most of us mumble or slur our words from time to time, especially if we're in a hurry or we're thinking about *what* we're saying and not *how*. With regular practice, though, you can improve here. However, it's also important not to exaggerate your enunciation, so that your speech sounds stilted and pretentious.

The last point to make about your voice is the importance of varying your pacing or timing. For most of us, this is natural—

TOOLS

Enunciation Timing

When you're making a key point or explaining something, you should speak more slowly. That's only logical. On the other hand, if you're giving an example that should be easy to understand, you can speak a little more quickly. Changes in timing not only allow you to adapt your speed to your message but also allow for refreshing variation.

except when we're nervous or excited. By practicing your presentation and maybe even recording it, you can figure out what sounds natural and appropriate for the points you're making.

One effective tool in presenting is the pause. It's a simple way to change pace. For example, you should pause briefly at the end of a sentence or a long phrase. But you should also pause before making an important point and after, for emphasis. If you know when to pause and for how long, you can help your audience better understand you—and you show confidence.

Warming Up

Presenters can learn some important lessons from performers. One of these lessons is the value of doing exercises to warm up the body and the voice. In their book, *Teaching and Performing* (Atwood Publishing, 1997), William M. Timpson, Suzanne Burgoyne, Christine S. Jones, and Waldo Jones recommend the following warm-up exercises.

Focus
- Sit comfortably, breathe deeply, and concentrate on feeling the air enter, fill your lungs, and leave.
- Focus on a sound silently repeated over and over.
- Think of the color spectrum, imagining each color one by one.

Body
- Rotate your head in half circles, from shoulder to shoulder, leaning your head forward and rolling from side to side, then repeating the motion with your head leaned back. (Never roll your head in a complete circle: a full

circle is an unnatural range of motion that stresses the upper vertebrae.)

- Tighten and stretch your face muscles, contorting your face, making exaggerated expressions.
- Stretch your back and legs, by bending at the waist and going up on tiptoe and raising your arms as high as possible.

Voice

- "Wiggle and waggle your lower jaw."
- Do tongue twisters, such as "Sally sells sea shells by the sea shore" and "rubber baby buggy bumpers."
- Repeat the following sound combinations: brrrr, ta ta ta ta, me me me me, us us us us, la la la la, ha ha ha ha, bee boy by beau boo, dee day die doe do ....

Setting Up

Arrive early, if possible. Then you can set up properly and not feel rushed. Stage fright is usually most intense in the first few minutes of being "out there." So, if you're busy getting things ready, you can be working through your nerves before you begin your presentation.

Check over the facilities. Test the lights and any equipment you'll be using and become familiar with the controls. The sooner you detect any problems or have any questions, the sooner you can call the contact person for help. Also, you definitely don't want to suddenly get stuck trying to figure out how to turn out the lights or turn on the equipment in front of a crowd.

Position your equipment. Put up a test slide and try viewing it from the back of the room, from the sides, from corners, and from any seat from which visibility may be limited. (Make sure, then, to guide members of your audience away from those "cheap seats.")

Look around for anything that might get in your way—electrical cords, furniture, equipment, and so forth. If you can move them aside before your presentation, do so. If not, make a mental note so you avoid bumping into them or stumbling over them. It's great to start or end your presentation with a bang—but not by falling over a cord.

Verify that your notes are in proper order. Read through the beginning of your notes to refresh your memory and be ready to start off right. Make sure you have a glass of water.

If you're providing refreshments, set them out. If refreshments are being provided, check to make sure they're out.

If you have time left, greet participants as they arrive. This is a great way to start establishing rapport one by one and to get a sense of the mood of the people attending your presentation.

Finally, just before you begin the presentation, set out your watch on the lectern or podium or somewhere convenient, where you can check it periodically without being obvious.

Hospitality Pays

Smart Managing   Experienced presenters have found that refreshments have a payoff. People connect around food. Coffee and tea work well in the morning. Soft drinks and cookies work in the afternoon. Refreshments can serve as icebreakers and help create a feeling of caring hospitality.

First Impressions

The first 90 seconds of a presentation are crucial. According to Ron Hoff, author of *I Can See You Naked: A Fearless Guide to Making Great Presentations,* "Presentation is a skill where preparation and attitude are apparent almost instantly." Throughout this book we've focused on *preparation.* As soon as you enter the room, though, it's all about *attitude.* So ...

Start on time. This shows respect for those who are punctual and sends the message that you intend to make the best use of your time. Be enthusiastic and sincere.

Smile. Show that you're pleased to be there. It doesn't matter if you've got a great smile or not. Just show that you enjoy what you're doing—even if you're feeling nervous.

Introduce Yourself

You want to begin with the "great unknown"—you. The audience wants to know who's going to be doing the presentation.

So, introduce yourself.

Keep it short and to the point, but friendly. This establishes rapport and gives your audience a sense of your personality. The participants will want to know at least your name, what you do, your credentials, and why you're doing this presentation.

An essential part of introducing yourself and making a good first impression is *eye contact*. This is an important means of establishing rapport with an audience, communicating visually with your body.

Perhaps as much as the words of your introduction, eye contact connects you with your participants and shows that you're going to be presenting *to* them and *for* them, not just *in front of* them. Eye contact helps build a relationship of trust.

Let's Go

Then, start your presentation. Since you've memorized the first two minutes or so, you start strong, confident, and in control.

How Important Is Nonverbal Language?

We communicate in person on three levels. Professor Albert Mehrabian of UCLA has studied the relative importance of these three levels. His results are surprising:

- Verbal—our words: 7%
- Vocal—our voices (tone, projection, resonance, etc.): 38%
- Visual—our faces and bodies: 55%
  Although we tend not to think about our voices, they're providing 38% of what we're communicating—for better or for worse.

Begin by outlining the objectives of your presentation. Even if you don't have these on a slide, you need to establish the context immediately. Sure, they probably know why they're attending your presentation—but they'll feel better if you show that you also know why they're there. Just as important, a shared understanding of purpose helps create a sense of community. Set a positive tone from the start.

Get their attention. If you don't have a slide that's going to grab them and pull them into your presentation, you should start with a riveting statement of facts, an anecdote, or anything that's likely to make them want to focus all their energies on

Don't Discount Yourself

Although it's good to be humble, you should maintain a sense of confidence in the value of your presentation. Avoid opening with comments such as "Well, here goes nothing" or "I hope that you find it worth your while to be here"—even in an attempt at humor. Such comments convey nervousness and a lack of confidence that the audience is sure to pick up on.

you and your presentation.

Should you start with humor? Many presenters use humor to begin a presentation because it can make the audience feel comfortable, release any tension (for them and also for yourself), and build rapport.

However, humor can be very tricky. Some people are not very good at telling jokes. Some audiences don't respond well to jokes. It can also be hard to find a joke that's unfamiliar to your audience—and that's not likely to offend anyone. If you're not sure that you can use humor, don't try.

It's crucial from the start to be attentive to signals from the audience, signals that let you know how they feel and how they're perceiving you and your presentation. Do you sense tension? Do you sense resistance? Do you sense particular areas of greater interest? Do you sense a lack of interest? Do you sense fatigue or boredom? The best presenters know how to read the members of their audience.

Imagine the people in your audience asking, "So what?" (Remember the WII-FM from Chapter 2.) If you're not focusing on answering that question with whatever you do in your presentation, you may have trouble holding their attention.

All Joking Aside

Many presenters feel obligated to begin with a joke. Lani Arredondo, in her book, *Communicating Effectively* (McGraw-Hill, 2000), warns against this technique: "Never open with a joke." It's too easy to fail, she explains. The joke may be stale, the presenter may have no sense of comedic timing or may botch the punch line, the joke may offend somebody. She concludes, "You have more to lose and less to gain by opening with a joke. So don't."

Start Where Your Audience Is

Sometimes we become so involved in our specialty areas that **Smart Managing** we forget that others might have trouble getting into them and following what we're saying.

Some friends told me about a situation with their young son. When telling them about events, he had a habit of starting somewhere in the middle, which confused them. Then, they realized that he was so wrapped up in the event and his feelings that he wasn't sensitive to their perspective. So, they just suggested, "Tell us like we weren't there." That summed up their perspective in a way he easily understood and helped him become aware of the need to start at the beginning and make sure they followed. The moral of this story is to start your presentation from the perspective of your audience and then make sure they follow every step of the way.

Delivery

Delivery involves many factors. Among the most important are body language, movement, and language usage.

Body Language

How important is body language? Remember the research results mentioned earlier a few pages back: the visual/body language aspect of our total communication has the most impact in getting our message across—55%. So, it's certainly crucial to have your body working for you—or at least not against you.

First of all, stand straight, but not stiff. You should be relaxed, not rigid.

Don't lean on the lecture or podium. If you drape over it like you need support, you may appear tired and your behavior may be contagious. Be relaxed, be casual, but don't be lazy. You should radiate energy. And if you want to lean on a wall, tables, or chairs, do so casually, not as if you depend on them to remain upright.

Speakers who are expressive and dynamic use their hands and arms. Speakers who don't make gestures come across as stiff. And they certainly don't inspire the audience. So, how do you become more expressive and dynamic? Just let your body react to how you feel.

If you're interested in the content and in reaching your audience, your hands and arms should naturally express that interest. If you're enthusiastic about what you're doing, your hands and arms should show that enthusiasm naturally. Just allow your body to get involved in your feelings.

Use your arms, not just your hands, to emphasize key points. Make open hand gestures, toward your slides and especially toward your audience.

Those are some basic, simple suggestions. You'll gesture more naturally with experience and practice.

The Wrong Gestures

⚠️ **CAUTION!**

Here are some things to avoid with your hands and arms:
- Don't lock your hands in front of you, in what's known as the "fig leaf" position.
- Don't keep your hands behind your back.
- Don't clench your fists, except for effect, to make a point.
- Don't fold your arms.
- Don't play with a pen, a pointer, or other object.
- Keep your hands out of your pockets.

Movement

In general, it's good to move around the room. But there are some things to avoid.

Don't always hide behind the lectern, podium, table, chairs, or other furniture. If it's appropriate to the circumstance, come out from behind that furniture and move around the room or stage. If possible, "work the room and work the audience." Move appropriately and with a purpose. Don't move simply because you're nervous. Keep in mind that moving with meaning is a great way to put your nervous energy to work for you.

Your movements should be natural and support your words and the rest of your presentation. Don't draw attention away from a slide if that's where you want your audience to focus.

Don't move constantly, just as you would not speak constantly. Pause for effect. Stand still to make an important point. Above all, don't pace.

In general, don't stay anywhere too long, except around the front of the room. Also, don't hover over anybody. Respect the personal space of your participants.

As you move around, don't make participants squirm to follow your movements. It's good if they move a little, but too much will distract them from focusing on what you're saying. Finally, don't talk with your back to the audience. And don't move while participants are talking.

Language

When you speak, convey confidence and show interest in what you're presenting and in the members of the audience. Speak with feeling.

Use short sentences and short, simple words. Use the active voice (for example, "We tested the product" or "The marketing department drew attention to the problem"), rather than the passive (for example, "The product was tested by us" or "Attention was drawn to the problem by the marketing department"). A presentation is not a report or an article, with long, complex sentences and a formal style. Speak precisely and concisely. Make every word count. Repeat important points.

Emphasize the sense of shared experience and interest: use "we" rather than "you" whenever appropriate.

Speak slowly and clearly enough that everyone in your audience can understand every word. Make sure you don't run words together or trail off at the end of phrases and sentences. This is most likely to happen as you move or as you shift from slide to slide or end a section. Lazy enunciation not only makes it harder for people to understand your words but also tends to cause their attention to wane.

⚠ CAUTION!

Empty Fillers

Avoid fillers, such as "ah," "um," and "you know."

Try to detect empty phrases in your speech and minimize or eliminate them. They are distracting and get in the way of your content. On occasion, you might use an expression like "You know what I mean?" to check for understanding, but if you use it every few sentences, it quickly grows tedious and annoying.

Presentation Technicalities

There are a number of technical issues to keep in mind that will help make your presentation go smoothly. These include lighting, working with slides, your use of notes, scheduled breaks, and handouts. Let's review each of these.

Lighting

When you're using slides, don't turn off all the lights in the room. Use a dimmer, if possible, or leave some lights on. Your goal should be to set up lighting that will provide good resolution of your slides, allow your audience to still see your face, and reduce the possibility of anybody becoming drowsy or even dozing off.

> **Smart Managing**
>
> ### Who Turned on the Lights?
>
> While you might be tempted to turn the lights off to allow better viewing of slides, keep in mind that the price is that it can really break the mood and the flow of a presentation when you switch all the lights back on after some time in the dark. Get the lighting right so it contributes to and doesn't distract from your presentation.

Working with Slides

When you're showing a slide, alternate your attention between the slide and eye contact with the audience. Talk to your participants, not to the screen. Here's a good technique:

- Put up a slide.
- Move toward the audience.
- Stop.
- Make your point, with eye contact (and gesturing toward the slide).
- Pause and survey the audience.
- Move back to your notes and the slides for your next point.

While you're showing the slides, you want to spare your participants the effort of taking notes, minimize their anxiety about keeping up, and keep their attention on what you're doing maximized. So, if you've got the material on a handout, mention,

"The details are in the handout" or "I've included these facts on the handout."

Always face the audience while you're finishing your comments about a slide. Then pause to key up the next slide. That ensures that you don't trail off at the end of a comment. It also gives the audience a break, a chance to absorb what you've just presented and get ready for the next slide.

Working with Your Notes

If you're working from your slides, without any notes, it

> **⚠ CAUTION!**
>
> **Don't Make It Feel like Basic Training**
>
> A friend who joined the military described as "the most brutal part of basic training" what the recruits called "Death by PowerPoint." The trainer put them in a room, turned off all the lights, and presented one boring slide after the next. As you work through your slides, keep your delivery lively—and be sensitive to signs they— and you—are dying out there.

may be easier for you to focus on the audience. However, you should make sure that you don't allow the slides to carry the full weight of the presentation. If your memory is good enough to remember all the additional points and comments that you want to make to supplement the slides, great! Otherwise, you might find it practical to use notes.

It's better to have any notes on cards, rather than on sheets of paper. The most practical size cards are 5 x 7, which allow enough space but are easy to handle. Write out only key points and essential phrases and words. The notes should just keep you on track and help you avoid leaving out anything important. Be sure to number your cards; it can be very embarrassing to skip a card or get them out of order!

Maintain eye contact as you speak, glancing at your cards for words and phrases to guide you through your presentation. If you handle your cards inconspicuously, the audience will be watching you, not your notes.

If you decide to print out your notes on sheets of paper, it's best to have only phrases, not a full text. But if you write out your script, make it easy to use, so you don't need to stay glued to the page. A good idea is to print it in large type, such as 14 or 16 points. A common practice, then, is to mark it up, using a single slash (/) for a short pause and two slashes (//) for a longer pause or to indicate phrasing and to remind you to look up frequently to establish eye contact. You may also want to use a highlighter pen to call attention to certain key words and phrases so you remember to emphasize them.

Don't forget to number the pages: it causes a big problem if you drop your script and have to shuffle through the pages to reassemble your text while members of your audience wait and fidget.

When we focus on main points and on information, it's easy to forget that a good presentation needs something else: *transitions.* There are the verbal signs of organization that show how the points and information are connected. Too often a slide presentation can become just a series of pieces: "This slide shows ..." and "Next we have ..." and "We end with a slide that ...." Transitions help audiences to understand how all of the pieces fit together. They also make a presentation flow more smoothly.

It's easy to develop transitions, since they're just a way of looking back and ahead. Here are some examples:

- "Now that we've covered the first advantage of working with us, experience with this market segment, let's move on to the next advantage ...."

TRICKS OF THE TRADE   **Marking Your Script for a Better Performance**
In his book, *The How-To of Great Speaking,* Hal Persons and Lianne Mercer recommend an elaborate method for marking a text for public speaking:
/   short pause
//   take a breath
X   end of thought
XX   long pause, look at audience
XXX   longer pause, take a breath, look at audience
<   raise your voice
>   lower your voice
The best system is whatever works best for you.

- "So far we've discussed telemarketing and direct mail. Next on our agenda is e-mail."
- "Our new version of this software has four major advantages over the previous version. The first is ...."
- "In conclusion, then, I'd like you to think about ...."

Transitions also help you avoid doing "the PowerPoint shuffle." That's when the presenter allows the slides to make the presentation and takes a secondary role, serving only to introduce each slide and then advance to the next. The tendency then is for the presenter to speak in a monotone and to hesitate to elaborate on the slides or interject a comment here and here.

Take a Break

We've already discussed the importance of scheduling at least one short break every hour or so. Sometimes the situation will suggest additional breaks, particularly if you present immediately after lunch or if your content is particularly difficult. Here are some suggestions for taking a break.

If you're presenting in an off-site facility, indicate the location of the bathrooms, phones, refreshments (if none are in the room), and support staff (in case anybody has a need or a problem).

Allow enough time for participants to use the bathroom, for phone calls, and for refreshments, but not so much time as to tempt participants to start other activities. When meeting on-site, it's so easy for participants to run back to their offices to check e-mail, dash off a few memos, or chase down a co-worker for a brief conversation. Wherever you meet, participants with laptop computers may try to finish reports, crunch numbers, or whatever. Then it's even harder to draw them back

Resume on Time

When you're ready to resume, don't wait for stragglers: it wastes time, doesn't show respect for the participants who are ready on time, and encourages conversations to develop or continue. Be professional in getting back to your schedule.

Smart Managing

into your presentation.

Handouts

If you've prepared handouts, you have to decide when you should hand them out. There are at least six options, each with advantages and disadvantages.

Set them out on the seats before the presentation.

- Advantages: easy, most convenient for the participants, least disruptive
- Disadvantages: takes time when you should be setting up and getting ready

Set them out in one or several piles near the doors.

- Advantages: easiest
- Disadvantages: some participants might miss them as they enter

Hand them out to participants as they arrive.

- Advantages: opportunity to greet one on one, convenient to close the doors at scheduled start time
- Disadvantages: takes time right before start, sometimes frantic as participants arrive in clusters

Ask someone to hand them out as the participants arrive.

- Advantages: easy, allows you to use the time to set up or to mingle
- Disadvantages: no opportunity to greet participants

Distribute as you're covering the sections or points to which the handouts refer.

- Advantages: timely, not distracting during earlier part of presentation
- Disadvantages: disrupts the flow, takes time away from your presentation

Pass them around at the end of the presentation.

- Advantages: not a distraction, you can refer forward to them during presentation

- Disadvantages: participants take notes that would be unnecessary if they had handouts

If you distribute handouts before you start or during the presentation, make sure they help, not hinder. Tell the audience when any points you're making or information you're providing is not on a handout, so they give their full attention to you. When you want them to refer to a handout, indicate the page and the section, then verify that all members of your audience are focused on the right part of the handout. Otherwise, you're sabotaging your efforts.

Manager's Checklist for Chapter 9

❑ Butterflies or stage fright or just plain fear is normal—but there are ways to reduce that feeling and make it work for you.

❑ "Dress for success" applies to presentations. If you know the people who will be attending your presentation, you should be able to dress appropriately and comfortably.

❑ Your voice can make a crucial difference in your presentations, from the very start. Develop it to use it most effectively.

❑ Arrive early and set the stage for your presentation. You'll seem more professional and you'll be less likely to encounter problems.

❑ The first 90 seconds of a presentation are crucial. Prepare to make the most of that time by starting strong and establishing rapport with the members of the audience.

❑ Know how to use body language, how to convey messages with your face, hands and arms, and movement and how to read the signals that participants are sending.

❑ Be prepared to deal with the technicalities of your presentation, including lighting, working with slides, using notes, taking breaks, and using handouts.

Handling Questions and Other Delivery Issues

How do you handle questions as part of your presentation? What do you do if something goes really wrong? That's what we'll talk about in this chapter.

Question Time

Not all presentations include questions, but if they do, you should be prepared. If you are, this can be the most stimulating and memorable part of the event for you and for your audience. What follows are some things to remember when dealing with questions.

The Big Question

When should you answer questions? There's no right strategy for all situations. It depends on the audience, the content, and the structure of the presentation, and your personality.

You can decide to take questions as they come up throughout the presentation. If so, you're far less likely to frustrate members of the audience who have questions early on. You can reduce misunderstandings and uncertainties, rather than allow them to develop. But it also takes more time and, if you're not really comfortable with handling questions, more energy. And it can take the presentation off track if you're not careful.

You can decide to leave time for questions and answers at the end. That way you don't have to deal with interruptions. But you may find yourself surrounded by participants with questions as soon as you announce a break. Also, if your presentation is structured to build up their knowledge to a culmination, an action point, you may have a faulty foundation and not realize it until the end.

You can decide on a compromise: pause after major sections of your presentation to take any questions. Also, if you do so just before a break, you create a natural opportunity for shy individuals to approach you during a break or for those interested in following up on questions raised.

Planning for the Questions

For some people, the hardest part of doing a presentation is handling questions. If they're already nervous, this is the most likely time for the butterflies to suddenly rise up again and go crazy.

The key is to maintain control of the situation. To do so, you need to be ready. Here is a five-step process for handling questions:

- Anticipate the questions that might come up.
- Listen carefully to the questioner.
- Repeat or rephrase the question.
- Answer clearly and concisely.
- Go to the next question.

Anticipate the Questions

Don't just trust your luck, assuming that you'll be ready and able to answer any questions. Prepare in advance. You know the content of your presentation, the objectives, and the participants, as discussed in Chapter 1—background, experience, needs, and interests. So, put yourself in their seats. What questions would you ask?

Jot down the questions most likely to come up, one to a note card. Then, go through them, one by one, and think about how you should answer each question. Jot down the essence of a good answer. You don't need to write out complete answers or memorize them. You'll be prepared and your answers will flow naturally and spontaneously, but professionally.

Then, any time you have a moment or two before you give your presentation, pull out the cards and review your questions and answers. This is an excellent way to calm your nerves, continuing to prepare instead of just worrying.

This preparation should help you be ready for any questions and to anticipate them with confidence. Show your confidence by using open hand gestures toward the audience when you ask for questions. Show your confidence also by waiting for them confidently, your arms relaxed at your sides. Don't fold your arms: that signals that you don't really want questions.

If participants are reluctant to ask questions, you can turn the tables and ask them to answer one or more of your questions. Allow enough time for them to think; counting mentally to five or 10 slowly should be enough.

If participants are tentative, encourage them. After all, it's not a quiz, just a way to help them realize what questions they should be asking. This strategy generally works well if they feel like they've gotten all of the content. You'll probably uncover some difficulties, gaps, or misunderstandings. Then, some members of your audience will likely start asking questions.

If not, what do you do? That depends.

Smart Managing

Preparing in Advance

Preparing questions in advance not only helps your confidence, it also makes you ready in case no questions come up immediately when you invite them.

You might just say, "Either that's the best presentation ever or you're the smartest audience." That comment may loosen them up a little and start the flow of questions. Or you could say something like "Well, if I were sitting out there, I'd want to know ...." and bring up one of the questions you've prepared.

The Card Method

TRICKS
OF THE
TRADE

If you've got a break coming up, you could try this approach. Distribute index cards at the break and ask your participants to jot down any questions they might have. Collect these at the end of the break and resume your presentation by going through the cards, reading each question, and answering it. This would be particularly appropriate if you suspect that members of your audience might be reluctant to ask questions in front of coworkers or strangers, either because they're shy or because of political or cultural reasons. The result is that you answer their questions under the cloak of anonymity.

If they seem tired or eager to take a break, obey one of the basic rules about asking for questions: don't do it. You might be able to wring a few questions out of them, but even the best answers in the world are unlikely to have much effect on them. If you're unsure, just ask them if they need a break. Then you won't be wasting time for minimal results and they'll appreciate your sensitivity.

If they seem alert and comfortable, don't do anything. You've given them ample opportunity, they seem to understand what you've presented, and you've varied the pace of your presentation. So, just say, "OK. I think we're all ready to get back to the presentation."

Some presenters, if they suspect in advance that they won't get many questions, set some up. They plant a friend or a colleague in the audience with a question or two. This strategy can be risky, because if anybody recognizes that the inquisitive "participant" is not one of them, it could undermine your rapport. On the other hand, if it's staged in such a way as to be obviously a plant, there's no sense of deception and a good laugh may get the ball rolling.

Listen Carefully

When someone begins to ask a question, focus on that person. Your eye contact shows respect and attention. Listen to the whole question before you start to answer. Otherwise, you'll likely seem rude. You'll certainly seem to not care about the audience. And you could be very embarrassed when you give a great answer, only to have the person respond, "But that's not what I was asking."

In fact, listen to the whole question before you even think about the answer. Sometimes questions wander around or take a sudden twist, to end up somewhere that the answer you're mentally formulating won't go. However, if the participant is fumbling to get the question out, you can tactfully intervene to help him or her phrase it. But then, be sure to verify that the end result is indeed the question the participant was trying to ask.

Repeat or Rephrase

There are at least three reasons to repeat or rephrase a question:

- to verify understanding
- to maintain control of your emotions
- to buy time to think about the answer

It's easier to maintain your poise and not allow your voice to betray any negative emotions if you first repeat or rephrase the question before answering it.

If someone makes a statement rather than asking a question, you can either ask him or her to rephrase it as a question or you can do it yourself. It's simpler if you do it yourself—if the statement-to-question conversion is straightforward. Otherwise, just ask, "What is your question?"—but without letting it sound like a challenge or a rebuke.

A participant says, "It doesn't seem practical to use this program to track all of our activities."

What do you do?

- You can rephrase that statement: "The question is 'Is it practical to use this program to track all of our activities?'" or "You want to know if it's practical to use this program to track all of your activities."
- You can ask the participant, "What is your question?"

The do-it-yourself approach is generally safer than asking for the statement in question form, for two reasons. First, the participant is likely to think that you're quibbling over the *form* when what really matters is the *content*. (For some, this may evoke bad memories of elementary school teachers.) Second, the participant may take your response as an evasion and so hit even harder: "I just want to know how anybody with any brains could expect us to use this stupid program when we're already too busy doing our jobs! That's my question!"

Obviously, it's easy to quickly slip into some negative energy. If you rephrase the statement, you control the language, and you're less likely to have a Q&A go bad.

Some presenters react to each question with a positive comment, such as "Good question!" Although this reaction can make the questioner feel more at ease and encourage others to raise questions, it can quickly lose its value. Let's face it: not every question is great. And even if you're lucky enough to get only great questions, you don't want to react to each of them in exactly the same way. Also, some people might get the feeling that you're using your comment just to buy time to think.

> ### It's Not Personal
>
> **Smart Managing**
>
> When you get a negative or hostile question, don't take it personally. The individual obviously has an ax to grind, and it usually doesn't have anything to do with you. Don't second-guess the questioner, just deal with the question in a forthright manner, giving the best answer you can. Don't ever get defensive. It just reinforces the negativity.

So, try varying your positive reaction. You could vary the wording: e.g., "That's an excellent question" or "Hmmm, you're going to make me work here!" You could vary the timing: react immediately or react after repeating or rephrasing the question.

No matter what, keep your reactions positive. To paraphrase that age-old advice: "If you can't say something nice about a question, don't say anything at all." Remain positive—even if for no other reason than to help keep calm, poised, and confident.

What if the question is vague? Here's what Marian K. Woodall, author of *Thinking on Your Feet* (Professional Business

Communications, 1996), says about that: "Often a question is virtually unanswerable because of the kind of question it is—long, winding, complicated, multi-faceted, or obscure. ... Don't try to answer a vague question because there is no way you can please the seeker. Get a better question." She suggests one of the following tactics:

- Ask to have the question repeated.
- Ask a question of your own.
- Ask for clarification.
- Ask for a definition.
- Clarify or define a point yourself.

To handle such questions, you have to keep in mind these tactics, but you also have to be able to sense the attitude of the person, the concern behind the question, and concentrate on resolving the situation.

Answer Clearly and Concisely

Every question in a presentation can become an important turning point. Usually, it all depends on how you deal with it.

Stay calm. Be open to the opportunity to help your audience better understand what you've presented—or to indicate what you should cover in the time remaining. Above all, don't let any question cause you to lose your poise—and perhaps the positive sense of community and rapport you've developed.

Don't rush to answer. Give yourself enough time to answer intelligently, articulately, concisely, and professionally.

Taking a little time to start answering shows that you're thinking. In fact, you should generally avoid answering as quickly as possible. It suggests canned responses—or little thinking. Woodall notes in *Thinking on Your Feet* that a pause does more than allow you a little time to think:

A pause can be considered oral *white space*, time surrounding a key idea in the way white space in an advertisement surrounds and thus emphasizes a key point. A pause also commands attention for what follows.

When you answer, focus your answer on the question: don't talk around it or overload the answer with superfluous information or verbiage. Above all, don't just repeat what you said during the presentation. Repeat key points, yes, but with explanations or examples. If your words didn't convey your message the first time, will simply repeating them work better the second time?

Support your answer briefly. If any participants want more support, they'll ask—or you'll sense it from their reactions to your answer.

If your answer is complex, structure it around points. Begin by stating, for example, "There are three issues involved here" or "Depending on the specific situation, there are four courses of action." Then, count off the points one by one (using your fingers as visual cues) as you make them.

Choose your words carefully. Among the winning entries in a contest for the worst analogies ever written in a high school essay was the following: "Her vocabulary was as bad as, like, whatever." Unfortunately, many of us occasionally fumble around for the right word or settle for something less.

If you've prepared for your presentation by anticipating likely questions and formulating good answers, you're probably going to find that the right words come more easily. If you still have trouble coming up with the right words, don't panic. It happens to all of us—with the possible exception of William F. Buckley.

Just apologize. Anybody who's ever been in your shoes or endured an oral exam will empathize. Recover and try to do better with the next question.

Avoid the Three D's

In her book, *Communicating Effectively*, Lani Arredondo warns against three reactions in answering questions:
- Don't *defend*. Getting defensive creates an adversarial relationship that can only hurt your relationship with the audience.
- Don't *debate*. If you get into a one-on-one competition, you'll leave the others behind or split the audience into factions.
- Don't *disparage*. Never act as if a question is bad, stupid, or otherwise undeserving of a good answer. You'll hurt the person's feelings and probably create a chilling effect that will stifle the other participants.

When somebody asks a question, maintain eye contact for the length of the question and the start of your answer, then look around at the other members of your audience. A question may come from one person, but the answer should be for all.

What if you don't know the answer to a question? The best advice is not to act like you do—you'll probably get caught and you'll lose your credibility. The best reaction may be to admit that you'll don't know and offer to check on the question and to report back to the participants. This works, of course, only if you'll have an occasion to meet with them again. You can also give the answer later to the person who arranged for your presentation, to pass along to the group.

You could also call upon the knowledge and expertise of others in the room. However, in doing this, you need to be careful not to lose control of the Q&A session. And if you don't know the group, you don't whether you can trust the "expert" who offers the answer.

Go to the Next Question

As you finish answering a question, you should be looking around the room. That's a signal that you've finished your answer and you're inviting other questions. And the participants should be signaling back to you. Maybe a hand is raised, an obvious signal. Maybe you notice that somebody is fidgeting, eager to speak.

What if the same person wants to continue? If he or she has another question, answer it. Then try to move on to others. If it's the same question, you should point out that you've already answered the question as well as possible and you expect that others have questions, too. If the person insists on pursuing the same question or following up on your answer, you have two options. First, if enough others seem interested, tell the person, "OK. How about one follow-up question and then we move on to another question?" Second, if you sense that interest in that question is low, offer to meet during the next break or after the presentation, with that person and anybody else who's interested, to discuss it further.

Especially if you're taking questions during your presentation, don't allow the Q&A to go on for too long. How long is "too long"? Watch the participants and read their expressions and body language to gauge their interest.

When it seems that interest has declined appreciably, simply announce that you'll be glad to take any remaining questions during the break, at the end of the presentation, or after.

When a Question Is More than a Question

Some "questions" aren't questions at all, but rather statements or even objections that aren't intended as requests for information, an explanation, or an opinion. They're challenges. If possible, rephrase the statement as a question. Then, you can provide an answer. You may even defuse any negative feelings with a humorous approach.

For example, imagine that someone "asks," "You're a moron if you think we're going to use any of this stuff!" Brutal. You then turn the statement into a question: "So, you're asking me, 'Are you a moron?'" You pause a moment, especially if members of the audience laugh, then answer (to the whole audience, not just the individual), "Well, I'd hate to take a vote on that right here and now" or "I'm not a psychiatrist, so I'm not qualified to evaluate my mental level." Your poise should turn a tough situation to your advantage.

You can prepare better for a difficult crowd than for difficult individuals, because you should be able to predict general attitudes toward the presentation and predict general reactions.

It's more difficult to prepare for the individuals who hit you with "question sharps." But, if you handle the questions as if they were asked sincerely to get an answer, you're likely to have the other members of the audience on your side. And sometimes a lack of peer support for the challenger or even a show of peer pressure against the challenging behavior may be enough to quiet that individual or at least take the edge off his or her attitude.

If a question is hostile, don't treat it as you would a normal question. Don't repeat it. Don't allow negative language and feelings a place in your Q&A. This only reinforces the negativity. Instead, do your best to neutralize things by rephrasing the question.

Let's take an example. Somebody speaks up: "This company has a history of exploiting its employees. Now they want us to change over to this new system, which will increase our work for no extra pay. How do you feel about being used to indoctrinate us to accept the new system?" Suddenly you're facing a sticky situation. Rephrase the challenge as a neutral question, to shape it constructively: "Your question, then, is 'Can you explain the advantages of the new system for employees?'"

Pause for a moment to allow the others to adjust to this shift in focus. Then, answer the question.

As you finish your answer, indicate that you're moving on to the next question, by walking away from the hostile participant and scanning the audience for a new question. Your body language sends the message loud and clear.

Sometimes the negativity may be pervasive. In that case, you may decide after another question or two that it would be best to wrap up the Q&A. Announce that you'll take one final question. Again, your message should come through loud and clear.

Dealing with Disasters

What's the worse that could happen during your presentation? If you can think about potential disasters and be mentally and emotionally prepared, you've got less reason to fear them.

Here are some examples of disasters your list might include:

- You find out that the time allotted has been reduced.
- The equipment fails.
- You tell a joke that falls flat.
- You get nervous and flustered and lose track of where you are.
- You stumble over a chair or trip over a cord.
- A fire alarm goes off.
- You suddenly become ill.

These are just a few things that could go wrong. After you've completed your list, go through the situations one by one and think about strategies for handling each situation.

The first part of any disaster strategy should be to not panic. Usually, a good laugh will break the tension—especially if some of the members of the audience react to the disaster with nervous laughter or an anxious silence.

So, let's consider the disasters listed above, as examples, with some suggestions for surviving and recovering.

You find out that the time allotted has been reduced. At the very worse, you can make your main points, support them with the essentials, ask and answer the most likely questions on your list, and then open it up for additional questions. Allow just enough time to do your conclusion.

The slide equipment fails. You know the saying, "The show must go on." Apologize to the audience and then add something like "Now, return with me to a distant past, before PowerPoint, when all we had for presentations was our notes and perhaps a blackboard or flip chart." Then, make the most of your primitive tools.

You tell a joke that falls flat. Ouch! Just shrug your shoulders

Go with What Works

A recent ad on TV showed a young businessman at a computer trying to a pull a file off the network and talking to tech support. The technician reports that the network is having trouble and suggests that he "go with Plan B." The man is stunned. "Plan B? I don't have a Plan B."

Then you see him in a glass-walled conference room with three people next to him of increasing height. He's saying, "So, as you can see, our profits grew from last year to this year and we expect an even bigger increase for next year. Any questions?"

The point, of course, is to have a Plan B. However, although the improvisation of a human bar chart is a failure, it shows an ingenuity that should inspire any presenter.

If your equipment fails, improvise!

and apologize: "I'm sorry. I got that joke at a Henny Youngman clearance sale." (You can choose your own comedian.)

You get nervous and flustered and lose track of where you are. Figure out where you are from your slides and notes. If you can't, just be honest: "My brain has derailed. Who can back me up so I can get on the track again?"

You stumble over a chair or trip over a cord. Just get up, dust yourself off, summon up what remains of your dignity, and laugh at your misfortune, with a comment such as "And the entertainment is free" or "This is the last time I work with a choreographer!"

A fire alarm goes off. File out according to the established procedure, just like back in elementary school, or use your common sense. As you and the participants wait for the official word, conduct a Q&A. Some may groan and resist, but it's a good opportunity for you to find out about their major concerns or areas of interest. Take notes, so you'll be sure to cover at least those concerns and areas if you lose some of your allotted time.

You suddenly become ill. Maybe it's a sudden case of the 24-hour flu or you had some bad seafood for lunch. The key question is whether it's best to stop (and later reschedule) or to try to carry on. Be honest and be smart. If you decide to continue, minimize your movements and conserve your energy. The participants should empathize with you and appreciate your commitment to them and your determination. They'll also understand if you suddenly make a mad dash for the door.

These are just a few disasters and a few suggestions for dealing with them. After you try this exercise with a few disasters, you'll probably feel more comfortable and confident that you can deal with almost any disaster.

If you're prepared for anything that could happen, you'll be confident and maintain your poise—and probably impress your audience with your professional manner.

Timing Is Everything

When you practiced your presentation, you noted the time necessary for each part. Then, you calculated the time for each checkpoint along the way, based on your scheduled starting time. You know, then, that when you finish the first part, it should be 1:12, the second should end at 1:23, the third at 1:31, and so on. Here's where the scheduling pays off: you know at any checkpoint whether you're likely to end on time or not.

Check the time surreptitiously—obsession with time is easily contagious. If you're looking at your watch or the clock, it's inevitable that someone in the audience will do the same, and then another, and then ... on and on. So, periodically, sneak a peak.

If you're off schedule, don't panic. There's nothing sacred about even the perfect presentation. If you need to end at a specific time, you can adjust your plans.

If you're running behind, make a mental note of things you can cut and things you can shorten. You can also cut as you go, although that's usually more difficult. You could change slides a little more quickly than planned. You could drop an example here and there. If you've scheduled a break, take it—but shave a few minutes. If you were planning to stop for questions, skip the Q&A and handle all questions at the end.

If you're running ahead, don't feel complacent—and, above all, don't waste time. It's OK to end your presentation early and allow extra time for questions. That's smarter than to lose time here and there and risk running over the allotted time or not giving your audience the opportunity to ask question. Most presenters would agree that presentations tend to take more time than planned, not less time. But it might be nice to break for questions or just to stand and stretch. The audience will appreciate it.

Close ... and Open ... and Close

The first rule of presenting: end on time. Don't presume that you can take more time from your participants than allotted or that finishing your presentation is more important than whatever they've got scheduled next.

Perhaps the best way to end a presentation is in three steps:

1. Recap your main points.
2. Invite questions.
3. Conclude.

In other words: close ... and open ... and close.

Recap Your Main Points

This should be easy. After all, you kept your main points in mind while preparing your presentation. In fact, you've probably got them on an agenda or recap slide.

Invite Questions

We've already discussed how to handle questions. The only difference, really, between Q&A during the presentation and Q&A at the end is that when you finish with questions you need to watch the clock, to allow enough time for your conclusion.

End your presentation as you began it: strong. That means that you don't just stop when the audience stops asking questions. You need to end with an effective conclusion—even if it means cutting the Q&A session short.

Conclude

End with a bang. You don't need to go on for more than a few minutes to recap the points of your presentation. The audience may grow restless. If you can sum up each point in a

Focus on the Key Points

Smart Managing   A presentation is not like a report or an article. You can't just present a lot of information and assume that you've done a good presentation. People can read a report or an article until they understand all the content. In a presentation, however, you've got just the set amount of time to get through to your audience. What matters is the effect at the moment. In other words, the presentation is not what you deliver, but what the members of your audience take away.

short, memorable phrase, it will have a greater impact. The phrase can be even more memorable if you repeat it.

If you want to have the participants evaluate your presentation, we devote the final chapter of this book to suggestions for doing so. You should also take a few moments after the participants have left and you're winding down to think about your presentation and make some notes for improving, while it's still very fresh in your mind.

Manager's Checklist for Chapter 10

❑ Prepare for questions—and know how to maintain control of the Q&A no matter what happens.

❑ Anticipate disasters, so you can prepare for them.

❑ Pay attention to time and make sure your presentation finishes when it's supposed to finish.

❑ End strong, so the main points of your presentation remain in the minds of the participants.

Evaluate, Learn, and Improve

How well did your presentation go? That's the bottom line. It's important that you feel positive about the experience— "I think I did a good job"—and that you believe that the participants also felt positive about it—"and people seemed to react well." But don't stop there. After all, what really matters is what the participants got out of what you did and how it will affect what they do in the workplace. So you should focus on the essential question: How effective was my presentation?

In some cases, the best way to determine the answer to that question is to facilitate a test of knowledge as a close to the meeting. Again, depending on your position with this team, your can take any of several approaches to testing what participants have learned from your presentation.

Direct Reports

If the participants are direct reports of yours, a written test is a great method for determining the effectiveness of your presentation. Also, in doing this, you set the pace for your next meeting. Your participants will expect a test at the end of the meet-

---

Takeaways Are Critical

TRICKS OF THE TRADE

You never want your direct reports walking away from a meeting feeling that they really did not learn anything. Everyone has a full schedule; when they take time out of their schedules to attend a meeting and then get nothing to add to their professional toolbox, engaging them in future meetings will be a struggle. Testing at the end of a meeting is a great way to make sure they learned something they can use. In fact, it might just take that final review of the content that will make something click for several of the participants.

---

ing, so they may interact better and be more attentive at that next meeting.

Clients and Customers

If you're an outside presenter, a written test might not go over very well. So, make it fun! Play a game with the content you've just covered.

One of the easiest ways of doing this is to break the audience into groups of four to eight participants. Then tell them to put away any materials you gave them or any notes they made. Have each group come up with a name and nominate a scribe. Then, you ask questions and the groups deliberate and come up with an answer, which the scribe writes down. Next, ask the first group to present its answer. If they're correct, ask the other groups to show their answers, so you can keep score. If the first group has an incorrect answer, move on to the next group, until you get the correct answer. Rotate around the room, letting each group have the first opportunity to answer a question. If there's no correct answer, have the groups go to their notes or materials to find the correct answer. If they still come up empty, provide the correct answer and explain where this was in the presentation. Ask some questions that call for answers with two or more parts, to make it even more challenging.

Questioning the Questions

You can also judge your presentation by the types of questions participants asked. Here are some ways to look at the types of questions.

If you finish and they have no questions, no matter how hard you prod, you need to ask yourself the following questions:

- Did I present the material in a way that caused the participants to really stretch their thinking to a higher level?
- Did I show that I was open to questions and comments?
- Was my presentation too long? Did I lose the group's interest?

If you get several questions on one specific section of your presentation, you obviously need to revisit the content of that section and the way you presented that content:

- Was the content relevant and appropriate for their needs, experience, and understanding?
- Did I organize the information properly and present it clearly?
- Did I provide examples?

Sometimes you'll get questions that will seem to be coming out of nowhere. They're somewhat related to the topic of your presentation, but not related to anything you presented. Here are a couple of things to think about:

- Should I have answered these questions in the context of my presentation? Should I address them in future presentations on this topic?
- If the questions are not related to my presentation, was there a miscommunication of what I was going to present?

Sometimes, particularly with outside presentations, participants may expect you to answer certain questions—and you're not aware of those expectations. This is why it's crucial to review the objectives of the presentation. After you review the objectives, someone may ask why you won't be covering a specific topic. Then you can address that expectation up front, rather than allow the misunderstanding to continue, only to surface as questions during the presentation or at the end.

It's very important to be able to read your audience by the

questions participants ask during the presentation—and the way others react to each of those questions. If you can identify areas of interest or concern, detect and diagnose misunderstandings, and determine the extent of any problems, you can really engage participants more fully because you'll be able to adjust the presentation as you go to better meet their needs.

Did You Meet All of the Meeting Objectives?

Refer back to the objectives of the presentation. Go through each objective and get feedback from the participants on whether or not you met that objective. Remember: what's most important here is how the participants feel. Yes, it's important that you feel that you met the objectives, but more important is what the participants have to say.

If the group feels that the presentation didn't meet an objective adequately, see if there's time left to revisit the topic, to review the information and answer questions until the participants understand better. In some cases, this will not be possible. If not, then consider sending additional information to the participants as a follow-up to the meeting.

After all the time and effort that you put into developing your presentation, don't allow yourself to fall short of your goals. If it requires more time and effort to ensure success at the close of a meeting, it's your responsibility to make it happen.

Don't Get Defensive

Getting defensive about the feedback and arguing about it is not a good use of your time. Just take note of all comments and suggestions. There are two good reasons to do so. First, of course, the notes will ensure that you won't forget or misunderstand the feedback. Second, focusing on writing down the feedback helps you overcome the very human impulse to explain, justify, and defend yourself. Just verify that you understand the comments and suggestions and keep good notes. Don't even think about them at this point. Save that for later, when you can relax and reflect calmly and objectively, away from the "heat of the moment."

Feedback Is the Breakfast of Champions

We all know that feedback can help improve what we're doing. And certainly it's easy to become so involved in developing and delivering a presentation that it's difficult to step back and evaluate the results and work on improving.

But we're all human, which means that it can be difficult to receive "corrective feedback," to accept and use "constructive comments" about what we've worked so hard to get right. So, we'll focus here on receiving feedback, on four recommendations for doing this effectively.

Rule #1—Don't Get Defensive

If you ask for the feedback, you've got to take what you get. You don't have to agree with it; in fact, it's probably better not to react at all. But you certainly want to avoid taking it personally, as an attack. If you do, you can bet you'll never get feedback from that person or from anyone who sees how you reacted to the feedback.

Try to forget all of the labels like "positive," "negative," "corrective," "constructive".... Simply take the feedback for what it is. Feedback, no matter what kind, is simply someone stating his or her opinion or perception of something you did or said. You should respect the fact that an individual is willing to communicate to you his or her perception.

Sure, you could argue, it's just a perception. But remember: perception is reality—at least in this case. When you try to reach someone, to communicate, to inform, you can't succeed except in terms of that person's perception. The only question open to debate would be how many participants in the group you need to reach in order to consider your presentation successful. That's up to you. But the key is that perceptions matter—and that you should accept feedback graciously.

You might be surprised at some of the feedback you'll get. One presenter got feedback that her nails were too long. Now, she didn't understand how that was relevant to her presentation, but that participant felt it was worth mentioning. So, should that presenter cut her nails? No, but she might want to accept the feedback as insight into her professional appearance. Remember: don't fight it; get what you can out of it.

Rule #2—Don't Try to Explain or Rationalize

When you get the feedback, don't make excuses or try to explain your side of the story. (Yes, this is very close to Rule #1, Don't get defensive. When we try to explain or rationalize, we step onto what for most people is a slippery slope.)

If, for example, the feedback is that the information from one section of your presentation was a little tough to follow, don't try to explain your thought process or make excuses as to why it did not come across as you had planned. The saying "It's the thought that counts" really doesn't work here. What matters is the result of that thought. Simply take the feedback and apply it to your next presentation.

Rule #3—Get Specific

Sometimes feedback is vague or general. You don't really understand it—and you're not likely to be able to use it to improve your presentations.

So, don't hesitate to ask the participant to clarify what he or she means, to give specifics. Now, this can be very difficult. For one reason, the participant may not be able to be specific or may feel uncomfortable doing so. For another reason, it may be hard for you to encourage the participant to be specific without coming across as challenging the feedback.

Just ask simple, open questions in a cordial, calm tone:

- When you said that the presentation was "weak," what did you mean? Could you give some examples where it was particularly "weak"?
- You said that the presentation was "poorly organized." Could you elaborate on that comment, please? Maybe you can remember where you first reacted to the organization.

By the way, don't emphasize the words that you quote, either with a pause, a change in tone, or those obnoxious "finger quotes" (a.k.a. "air quotes"). That emphasis could be interpreted as showing disrespect for the participant and his or her feedback.

Be tactful and don't push it. If you can't easily help a participant be more specific in his or her feedback, just let it go. Also, don't suggest specifics—"Do you mean that I didn't give examples? Did you mean that my slides were primitive?" That's "leading the witness": it's great if you want to be in control, but that defeats the purpose of asking for feedback.

Also, don't tamper with the words used by the participant. For example, if she called the presentation "weak," don't use other terms, even if they seem synonymous: "Could you tell me why I seemed hesitant?" or "Could you give some examples where I fumbled for facts?" Stick with the participant's exact words and let him or her elaborate on them.

Rule #4—Thank Them for the Feedback

Remember that giving feedback is sometimes more uncomfortable than receiving it. So, as you get feedback, make sure that you thank the participants for their input and for the effort. First, they're helping you improve. Second, they're taking a risk to do so.

It's especially important to express your appreciation when you're dealing with people who directly report to you. When you ask for their feedback and get it, it's most important to thank them and then make a change based on their feedback. They will feel good that you paid attention to their opinions and they will have more confidence in themselves and in you as their leader.

These are very basic rules to follow. But they should help you make the

> **⚠ CAUTION!**
>
> **Don't Ask if You Really Don't Want to Change**
>
> Asking for feedback and getting it is really only half of the equation. Once someone has given you feedback, their expectation is that something will be different because of their feedback. If you don't make changes based on their feedback, at least let them know why not. And if you really don't want the feedback, you're better off not pretending to care enough to ask for it.

Four for Feedback

Here's a suggestion to help you deal better with feedback. Include in your script or pack of note cards a final sheet or card with the following:

• Someone is sharing a perception. Be gracious, not defensive.

• Simply take notes. Don't try to explain or rationalize.

• Get specific. Ask them to clarify, with simple, open questions in a cordial, calm tone.

• Thank them for the feedback.

As you reach the point in your presentation when you solicit feedback, set this sheet or card in front of you, to remind you to follow the four basic rules.

most of the opportunity to improve that you have with every presentation.

Most important, remember that you do not need to change everything that generates "corrective" or "constructive" feedback. Many times you will simply thank participants for their feedback and tell them you will think through how you will use that feedback in future presentations. Don't get defensive, don't make excuses, and—most of all—show appreciation for their honesty.

Working with a Survey

If you decide to use a survey, there are a few ways to make the most of this means of eliciting feedback.

• **Keep it short.** The more items, the more effort you're expecting ... and the less you're likely to get out of the survey. In general, it should take participants no longer than three minutes or so to complete the survey.

• **Phrase the items carefully and concisely.** Participants should understand what each item means immediately.

• **Give neither too few nor too many choices.** If you use a Likert scale, it's best to give three to five choices. If you ask for a rating, 1 to 10 allows more accuracy than 1 to 5 and is less complicated than 1 to 20.

• **Allow neither too little space nor too much for open-**

Likert scale A system for rating responses to a statement by choosing among points along a continuum, consisting of the two extremes and any number of equidistant intermediate points. The scale can range from the simple (two choices: e.g., "Agree" and "Disagree" or "Always" and "Never") to the complex ("Strongly Agree, Somewhat Strongly Agree, Less Strongly Agree, Somewhat Agree, No Opinion, Somewhat Disagree ...").

The term is named after Rensis Likert, who proposed this method in an article published in 1932, "A Technique for the Measurement of Attitudes."

ended questions or comments. If you want reactions, the amount of space that you leave indicates how much or how little you expect. A quarter inch is probably too little; a page is probably too much. Also, remember that handwriting will vary widely—and usually takes more space than we would estimate. If you allow too little space, you may get substantial comments, but you may need a magnifying glass to read them.

The Sample Survey Questions (sidebar) show how you can combine asking Likert-type questions and requesting comments to elaborate. There are also suggestions for interpreting the responses when participants do not leave comments.

If all goes well, you'll receive a lot of survey forms reporting "Highly Effective," "Strongly Agree, and "Too Much." That's good for the ego. But if you want to improve, you'll focus on the other responses, especially if you get a significant number of any one response. Those responses indicate the need to improve. And, if all goes well, you'll receive some thoughtful, specific, and articulate comments.

But what if the forms come in with the "Comments" spaces empty? Here are some suggestions, using the Sample Survey Questions, to guide you in "getting something out of nothing."

How to interpret "Not Effective" answers if no comments were added:

- Did you present the materials in a way that showed why

Sample Survey Questions:

1. How would you rate the effectiveness of the materials you received today?

Highly Effective   Effective   Not Effective

If "Not Effective," what should be changed?

2. The information was presented in a way that I understood and I will be able to articulate to others.

Strongly Agree   Agree   Do Not Agree

If you do not agree, why?

3. The amount of information given to me at this meeting was:

Too Much   Just Right   Too Little

Comments:

they are important and how the participants would benefit from the information given?

- Did you allow enough time for the participants to review the materials and ask questions?

How to interpret "Do Not Agree" answers if no comments were added:

- Review your agenda and try to pinpoint areas that took longer to present than you'd planned. Maybe you moved on to the next section too soon because you were concerned with time.
- Remember the different ways in which we learn. Did you present the materials in ways that would fit the different learning styles?

Your Turn

Diane DiResta, in her book *Knockout Presentations*, suggests that you evaluate your delivery, either by videotaping and viewing your presentation or from memory immediately after your presentation. She suggests using a 1-to-10 scale and provides the following criteria:

More Evaluation Questions

In her book, *Presentations*, Daria Price Bowman recommends asking the following questions:

- On a scale of 1 to 6 (with 1 being the highest), how would you rate the presentation overall? the content? the presenter? the visuals?
- If you were to give the presenter advice on improving the presentation, what two things would you recommend?
- What key points do you remember most?
- What aspects of the topic did the presenter leave out that might have been of interest to you?
- Why did you attend?

- Posture
- Purposeful Movement
- Image/Appearance
- Confident Language
- Eye Contact
- Gestures
- Intonation
- Enthusiasm
- Facial Expression
- Pausing
- Speaking Rate
- Non-words (ah, um)
- Uptalk (pitch rises)
- Q&A Control

She also suggests that you add any notes that might help you improve your next presentation.

Now What?

Now that you have feedback, what do you do with it?

If you're wise, you treat it as a gift, as an opportunity to improve your presentations. If you've received a lot of specific complaints and suggestions, congratulations! Just don't become overwhelmed. Organize the suggestions by dividing them into categories that make sense for your situation, such as the following:

- organization
- content
- slides
- handouts
- logistics
- delivery
- facilitation
- dealing with questions
- getting feedback

Keep It in Perspective

Throughout life, you will meet with adversity, probably including less than totally positive feedback on your presentations. Those things are not what will change your life. It's what you decide to do about those things that will change your life.

Smart Managing

Then, as you begin developing your next presentation, pull out the complaints and suggestions, category by category, and think about how you might use them to improve. As discussed earlier, these suggestions are perspectives: each is an individual opinion about how you did one specific presentation. So, use them to gain insights, to help you think differently. You don't have to accept and use every comment; just think about each and evaluate it. Then, use those that will help you do better next time.

Manager's Checklist for Chapter 11

❏ However you and the participants might feel about your presentation, the essential question is "How effective was the presentation?" What really matters is what the participants got out of what you did and how it will affect what they do in the workplace.

❏ The best way to evaluate the effectiveness of a presentation is by testing the participants.

❏ You can also judge a presentation by the types of questions participants asked.

❏ Get feedback from the participants on whether or not you met the objectives of the presentation.

❏ Follow four basic rules for accepting feedback: don't get defensive, don't try to explain or rationalize, get specific, and thank them for the feedback.

❏ A quick and easy way to get feedback is by having participants fill out a brief survey to rate the presentation by
selected criteria and offer comments.

❏ We should treat all feedback as perspectives that provide
us with insights and opportunities to improve.

Appendix

PowerPoint Quick Reference

Throughout this book, we provide tips and techniques on how to maximize PowerPoint. This appendix contains some of these tips plus many more. We've created it as a quick reference guide so these tips and techniques are easy for you to find and use.

PowerPoint 2000 Tips

Choosing the Proper Format
- To begin, choose File>New.
- In the New Presentation pop-up window, select the Presentations tab and pick a format that fits your objective.

Changing Your Background
- Decide if you like the current background and design. To change the background on all your slides, go to View> Master>Slide Master.
- From there, select Format>Background and the Background pop-up window appears.

- Select the drop-down arrow and choose More colors or Fill Effects.
  - More colors let you pick a color.
  - Fill Effects>Gradient allows you to fill the background with a gradient.
  - Fill Effects>Texture or Patterns gives you some other backgrounds. (Most do not provide a very good contrast.)
  - Fill Effects>Picture>Select Picture lets you add your own custom background.

Changing Your Slide Color Scheme

- Go to Format>Slide Color Scheme. Your Color Scheme pop-up window appears. This has two tabs in it. The first tab is Standard. These are the standard color schemes. If you want to customize your colors, click the Custom tab.

Make Logos and Design on Every Screen

- Go to View>Master>Slide Master.
  - Put any logos you want on the Slide Master by selecting Insert>Picture.
  - Set up the colors and sizes you want for the text here. Always do those tasks here, not on each individual slide as you work.
- If you are creating a slide and do not want the logo or image you put onto the Slide Master on that particular slide, go to...
  - Format>Background and the Background pop-up menu appears.
  - Click on the box at the bottom that says, "Omit background graphics from master."
  - Clicking Apply will apply this feature only to this slide. If you Click Apply To All, then the logo will not appear on any of the slides.

Animating Words and Objects

- You have some phrases on a screen and want the phrases to come up one at a time.

- Highlight them, then go to Slide Show>Custom Animation. This will bring up the Custom Animation pop-up window.
- The first tab Order & Timing handle how the animation is to happen.
- The second tab Effects is where you select the animation effect you want.
- The box in the upper left corner shows you everything on the slide that can be animated.
- The bottom left box shows you everything you've animated. You can single-click anything in this box the click the green up and down arrows to change the animation order.

Animating Charts
- Single-click your chart, then go to Slide Show>Custom Animation to the Chart Effects tab and animate the chart here.

Inserting and Handling WordArt
- Insert>Picture>WordArt or use the WordArt icon on the draw toolbar.
- You can size the words once you have them on the screen.
- You can animate the words.
- Not only can you fill WordArt with a solid color, but you can fill it with any Fill Effect (i.e., texture, gradient, picture).
- You can make the WordArt 3-D. Make sure to select Parallel under Direction on the 3-D Setting Toolbar.

Symbols
- Choose an AutoShape from the Draw Toolbar (usually located at the bottom of your screen).
- You can fill it with a solid color or any Fill Effect (i.e., texture, gradient, picture).
- You can make it 3-D or add a shadow using the icons at the end of the Draw Toolbar.

Linking to Another Presentation
- Create a box or use any text, clip art, or photo. (Anything not grouped can be used as a hyperlink.)

- Single-click on your object, then go to Slide Show>Action Settings and the Action Settings pop-up window appears.
- Decide if you want this link to happen on a Mouse Click or a Mouse Over.
- Select the appropriate tab, then select the radial button next to Hyperlink to.
- Select the drop-down arrow and choose what you want this link to hyperlink to.
- Click OK and then run the Slide Show to view your hyperlink.
- You can use this feature to link within the same presentation, run an application such as Excel, link to a Web site, etc.

Drawing a Straight Line
- To draw a straight line, hold down the shift key as you draw it.

Semi-transparent Symbols
- Select the symbol, right-click, and choose Format AutoShape. On the Colors and Lines tab, check the semi-transparent box. Click OK.

Transitions
- Make your transitions easy on the eyes and easy on your computer.
- Use any of the following:
  - Blinds
  - Box
  - Split
  - Stripes
  - Wipes

Do You Know About?
- Format Painter: Single-click the object you have formatted, i.e., a box with a gradient or a shadow, then double-click the Format Painter located to the right of the Paste icon. Click on any other object and it will take on the same attributes as the original.

- Animated templates: Pulse.
- Selecting a group: Place the mouse pointer above and to the left of the objects, hold down the left mouse button, and drag the rectangle around all the objects. Release the mouse and all the objects are selected. Go to Draw>Group and they will become one object.
  - Useful for grouping clip art.
  - If you select an object you do not want, single-click that one object while still holding down your Shift key.

Showing a Hidden Slide During Slide Show

- Before you advance to that slide, press the "H" on your keyboard while clicking to advance and your hidden slide will be shown.

Changing Your Default Font

- Make sure nothing is selected, then go to Format>Font and choose the font and point size you want. This will change the font that appears when you use the Text Box tool to add text outside of your bullet points.

Up and Down Arrow Keys

- Select an object and use these keys to move an object up or down or side to side.

Advancing Slides Manually or Automatically

- Slide Show>Set Up Show gives you the option to advance slides manually or automatically after a set amount of time.

Key Things to Always Check

- Slide Show>Set Up Show>Advance slides Manually.
- Slide Show>Custom Animation>Timing>Animate On mouse click.

Index